T0078260

LEFT SHIFT

How and why America is heading to
second rate, single payer health care.

DAVID N. ARMSTRONG, M.D.

ARCHWAY
PUBLISHING

Archway Publishing books may be ordered
through booksellers or by contacting:

Archway Publishing
1663 Liberty Drive
Bloomington, IN 47403
www.archwaypublishing.com
1 (888) 242-5904

ISBN: 978-1-4808-3396-8 (sc)
ISBN: 978-1-4808-3395-1 (hc)
ISBN: 978-1-4808-3397-5 (e)

Library of Congress Control Number: 2016913174

Print information available on the last page.

Archway Publishing rev. date: 09/29/2016

They are trying to sell you socialized medicine, and that is a bad product.

—Senator Phil Gramm, Texas,

The commercialization of health care is the primrose path down which inexorably lies American medicine—first-rate treatment for the wealthy and tenth-rate treatment for the poor.

—Dr. David Owens (MP), House of Commons,

To Blair, my wife

And my sons

Ross and Blake.

For all the late nights,

The early mornings,

Their patience,

And their love.

LEFT SHIFT

Left *(Engl.,adj)* c. 1200, "opposite of right," Old English **lyft* "weak; foolish" (in *lyft-adl* "lameness, paralysis"). Compare East Frisian *luf*, Dutch dialectal *loof* "weak, worthless").

Shift *(Engl., n.1)* c. 1300, "a movement, a beginning," from *shift* (v.).

Left shift *(Medical definition)*

A hematological response to overwhelming sepsis, wherein a disproportionate number of immature leucocytes (white blood cells) are released by the bone marrow to combat invading bacteria.

Left shift *(Political definition)*

A shift in political direction, whereupon a society adopts more liberal or socialist policies, turning aside free market principles.

CONTENTS

PREFACE

"UNIVERSAL COVERAGE," "NATIONALIZED HEALTH CARE," "socialized medicine": it is the utopia of free medical for all. But how just how good is "socialized medicine"? For half a century, Britain has enjoyed the most comprehensive form of socialized medicine in the Western world, time enough for its effectiveness to be evaluated.

This book compares, head to head, Britain's National Health Service (NHS), the icon of socialized medicine, with US medicine, the paradigm of free market health care. It compares the number of procedures performed, the cost of performing each procedure, and outcomes (death rates) for each. No such comparison has previously been made, and harsh truths emerge.

The cost data provide an enticing argument for nationalized medicine: Health care costs in the United States are over three times those in the United Kingdom, over $9,000 for every man woman and child in America compared to a frugal $3,000 in Britain. Not unexpectedly, the United States boasts twice the number of physicians and twice the hospital beds. Americans undergo twice the number of surgeries, at an average of one and a half times the unit cost.

How do the outcomes compare, and what do we use as a yardstick? Some deaths are preventable by early detection; for example, breast cancer by screening mammography, colorectal cancer by screening colonoscopy. By this measure, the United Kingdom lags significantly: death rates from breast and colorectal cancer in the United Kingdom are almost twice the rate in the United States.

Heart attacks (ischemic heart disease) are the commonest cause of death on both sides of the Atlantic, yet the problem consumes disproportionate resources in the United States. An American is seven and a half times more likely to have a coronary angiogram, and six times more likely to undergo coronary artery bypass graft surgery, while his transatlantic cousin makes do with his nitroglycerin pills. Return on this huge investment comes during an acute myocardial infarction, the critical moment when death may be averted. By this measure, the United States excels, with a death rate from acute myocardial infarction 50 percent lower than Britain.

The high-intensity, fast-paced nature of US health care can presently afford such luxuries as aggressive intervention for cardiac disease, technology-laden surgical procedures, and intensive screening for cancer. Meanwhile, Britain's cash-strapped NHS is overstretched in keeping up with today's emergencies, with precious few resources to avert tomorrow's tragedies. Although a US survival benefit can be demonstrated in the most common fatal diseases, this is only possible at enormous cost, borne, for now, by the health consumer. How long we were prepared to pay this premium previously depended on what the marketplace would bear. In the future, health care delivery will become subject to political whim, as health care delivery drifts inexorably to the left.

As the Affordable Care Act, or colloquially, "Obamacare," becomes a reality, health insurers are constrained by new requirements: No lifetime cap, no preexisting conditions, mandatory contraceptive provisions, outlawed risk-profiling, and a surfeit of elderly and sicker individuals. The remaining "big three" private insurers, condensed from a whirlwind of megamergers and acquisitions, survey their futures nervously in an increasingly hostile administrative and political environment.

In the public sector, sixteen of the original twenty-three health care cooperatives established under Obamacare are closed, and the remaining seven are insolvent. This brings with it a price-tag of $2.4 billion dollars, and leaves an estimated 800,000 Americans scrambling to find alternate coverage. Health care, private and public, is on a fast track to becoming a Lehman Brothers 2.0, when the health care sector will be on life support from the US taxpayer, and the US version of Britain's National Health Service will become a reality: "Free" for all, from cradle to grave. And accountable to none.

INTRODUCTION

AT MIDNIGHT ON JULY 4, 1948, THE BRITISH NATIONAL Health Service (NHS) was born. A child of necessity, the National Health Service was conceived during the darkest days of World War II when the future of Britain itself lay in the balance. The NHS was the centerpiece of Clement Attlee's radical postwar Labor reforms that enacted sweeping nationalization of British industries, bringing 20 percent of British industry under public ownership. Even the Bank of England, independent since before 1700, was herded into the public fold. The National Health Service was created in the likeness of the wartime Emergency Medical Services, which brought the municipal and voluntary hospitals under blanket government control, to handle the expected deluge of civilian casualties. Masterminded by the radical left-wing Labor MP Aneurin Bevan, the NHS went well beyond any previously considered health reforms and was to become the jewel in the new welfare crown, providing free health care for all Britons, "from cradle to grave, from duke to dustman."

Bevan, "a clever politician, never graduating to statesman," the British Medical Association lamented, sought both social reform and party political capital in his new creation. Rather than creating a national network of locally run and funded hospitals, as Churchill's wartime coalition government had planned, Britain's hospitals were brought under direct control of the Ministry of Health. Having nationalized the hospitals, their doctors and nurses were also delivered into state employment. Funded by His Majesty's Treasury through general income taxation, the purse strings of Britain's health were kept tight from the outset. Any liberalization of funding would be possible only by proportionally massive tax hikes, ballot-thin ice for any government to tread. Attempted cutbacks produced accusations of denying a traditional (after a half century, almost historic) right to free health care.

Bevan's goals did not stop at free and universal health care. He also sought to redistribute wealth by funding through general income tax. As a radical left-winger, he also sought to create a monument to the socialist state. Thus politicized, the NHS would become a parliamentary tar baby for three generations. Ironically, its founder himself was its first political victim: Bevan resigned in bad-tempered protest when, in 1951, the already cash-strapped NHS introduced charges for false teeth and glasses. He was the first of many who would step into the quicksand of Britain's new health service.

The NHS, first proposed in 1942, was instituted in all its glory only six years later, in 1948. By contrast, the closest US equivalents, Medicare and Medicaid, first proposed in 1946, would not see the light of day for twenty-two years, in 1968. Even these steps toward universal health care would not have occurred had it not been for the assassination of John F. Kennedy.

At the beginning of the century, the Supreme Court ruled government involvement in national health care as unconstitutional, a principle which would prevail until the

1940s. Even during the Great Depression of the 1930s and the creation of Roosevelt's sweeping nationalized programs, nationalized health care was considered too revolutionary. "The people are not ready" was Roosevelt's explanation. Harry Truman, spurred by Beveridge's plans for postwar welfare in Britain, was to meet with abject failure in his attempts to introduce a similar plan in the United States. The principal reason for Truman's failure was the unexpected postwar boom in America, a welcome alternative to the expected postwar depression. The sustained and ultimately successful opposition by the medical lobby helped drive the final nail into the coffin of US "nationalized medicine" for two decades.

Nationalized health care languished under Eisenhower, partly, according to his detractors, because of his insulation from medical costs through his military career. The marriage of his daughter to the son of Harvey Cushing, a prominent Yale neurosurgeon, did not help the cause of the national health advocates in America.

The election of John F. Kennedy breathed new life into the cause of a national health service, the centerpiece of Kennedy's New Frontier policy. Twice rejected by the Senate, his assassination in 1966 brought a turnaround in the mind-set of policy makers.

The landslide liberal shift of the Johnson era and the legacy of a martyred president brought about a reversal of the previous Senate rejection of national health plan. Wilbur Mills, chairman of the Ways and Means Committee, negotiated an all-encompassing compromise between the medical lobby, Congress, and the White House. The end result was the creation of Medicare, a federally funded health care plan for elderly

Americans, and Medicaid, a plan for the underprivileged. In August of 1968, Johnson traveled to Independence, Missouri, where he signed the Medicare and Medicaid laws into law with a now elderly Truman sitting in a wheelchair at his side.

In Britain, the National Health Service, macromanaged by the Department of Health and micromanaged by the Regional Health Boards, faced cash shortages from the outset. Waiting lists for surgery, and even to see a physician, climbed relentlessly. As the largest state employer, the NHS also carried the burden of managing over 1 million employees, the second largest employer in Europe (surpassed only by the Soviet Red Army). Intent on their own personal and collective welfare in the face of government restrictions, hospital workers and ancillary staff staged work-to-rules, overtime bans, and wildcat strikes to press their pay claims. The period from the 1960s to the 1980s was blighted by industrial unrest throughout the nationalized industries, including the health service unions. Surgical lists were canceled, wards were closed, and the waiting lists grew ever larger. The industrial unrest of the 1970s produced successive "winters of discontent" culminating in power cuts, a three-day working week, escalating unemployment, hyperinflation, and, ultimately, a change in government. Financed through Her Majesty's Treasury, NHS expenditure increased at a glacial 3 percent per annum, far below the double-digit figures in the United States.

For a half century, health care costs in Britain have remained around 8 percent of the gross national product, exceeding $3,000 for every man, woman, and child in 2015. In the face of expanding medical technology and an aging population, something had to give. As a result, more and more Britons found their names on the waiting list, a form of covert health care rationing from day one. In the United States, health care spending has escalated for fifty years, exceeding $3 trillion, or 17 percent of GDP in 2015, over $9,000 for each and every American.

In spite of relatively modest increases in NHS costs in the United Kingdom, Margaret Thatcher recognized the need to introduce market economics into the financial "bottomless pit" of the NHS. Ironically, advice was sought from the United States in the form of Professor Alain Enthoven, "a Vietnam-era Pentagon planner," a *Lancet* editorial noted anxiously. A taste of free market principles was introduced in the form of the "internal market," whereby general practitioners would refer to the most cost-effective hospitals for the treatment of their patients.

NHS hospitals, thus far unburdened by even the most basic financial data, rushed to produce figures illustrating their cost effectiveness. The new atmosphere of free market competition led to an actuarial "race to the bottom" by hospitals keen to advertise their abilities to provide health care at a lower price than their new competitors. Each hospital (now independent "trusts") calculated its costs to perform each of five hundred surgical procedures or treat diseases from heart transplants to sleep disorders. The figures, published as the 1998 "Reference Costs," included all the five million surgeries performed in England that year, covering five hundred disease categories. Significantly, the grand total amounted to only £5 billion in costs, far below the £30 billion NHS hospital budget. In addition, the cost of performing the same procedure varied widely from trust to trust, on average, by a factor of four.

Certainly, the "Reference Costs," although a step in the right direction, were gross underestimates of the true cost of performing the procedures, which led to an erroneous impression of cost effectiveness when comparing these figures with US cost data. The "sharp-elbowed" practices of the internal market would be reformed under Tony Blair's "New NHS," where hospitals were judged more on patient outcomes rather than financial performance. Publication of both financial data from the NHS, and morbidity/mortality data has, for the first time in its history, enabled a head-to-head comparison with other health care systems, in this instance with the United States.

Health care rationing has been the modus operandi in the NHS since its inception. The practice has been upheld by the courts even in the most heart-rending cases. In 1995, a ten-year-old girl, "Child B," became the poster child of NHS rationing. Having developed Hodgkin's lymphoma at the age of five, the child underwent chemotherapy but subsequently developed acute myeloid leukemia. The young girl underwent chemotherapy, radiation, and a bone marrow transplant, which produced a temporary remission. When the leukemia recurred, the child was denied a second (estimated $100,000) bone marrow transplant by Cambridge Health Authority, on the grounds that it would likely not be successful. The father, having sought advice from the United States, was told she might have a 30 percent chance of success, so took his child's case to court. Lord Justice Laws, hearing the case in the High Court, upheld the opinion of the father and ordered Cambridge Health Authority to go ahead with the treatment. The case went immediately to the Court of Appeal, where it was heard the same day, by Sir Thomas Bingham, Master of the Rolls.

The Appeals Court overturned the high court decision on the basis that the health authority had to make its decisions on the basis of limited resources and had acted "rationally and fairly."

"Difficult and agonizing decisions have to be made as to how a limited budget could best be allocated to the maximum advantage for the maximum number of patients. This is not a judgment the court can make," explained Sir Thomas. The publicity surrounding the case stimulated funding from private donors, and the treatment went ahead. "Child B" died several months afterward.

This and other well-publicized episodes of overt medical rationing form the tip of the iceberg. The long waiting lists in Britain (estimated at 1.3 million in 1998 and 3.4 million in 2015) dissuade general practitioners (GPs) from referral to the hospitals, where a six- to twelve-month wait to see a specialist, followed by another six- to twelve-month wait for surgery would result in frustration and disappointment. Nonreferral or denial of care probably constituted the largest backlog of covert rationing in Britain.

In the United States, health care costs continued to escalate from the 1980s onward, reaching 13.5 percent of gross domestic product (GDP) in 1990. Health care inflation was out of control and threatened the whole economy, while 45 million Americans remained without any coverage whatsoever.

The remedy was offered in the form of the Clinton health plan, which placed much of the financial burden on employers, and proposed reined-in HMOs as the centerpiece of delivery. The plan was soundly defeated. Having escaped confinement on Pennsylvania Avenue, HMOs sought comfort on Wall Street, where they were greeted enthusiastically. A binge of megamergers and acquisitions followed, each one accompanied by CEO bonuses and severance packages the size of the health budget of a small nation: $990 million in one instance. It was to prove a short and unhappy marriage. Denial of care and limited access to HMO doctors bred growing resentment in the American public. Doctors faced decimated fee schedules and a blizzard of paperwork. Discounted health insurance premiums resumed their climb as HMOs lost money. Columbia HCA was raided by the FBI, for alleged dubious billing practices. Stock prices fell from their peak in the glory days of 1995 to half their value four years later. Tobacco-style class action lawsuits from denied patients waited in the wings. The only smiling faces were the now-retired CEOs. America had run down the primrose path of managed care to find itself at the same impasse it faced a decade earlier.

Though frequently lacking long-term solutions, US medicine does not lack for men and materiel. Medical manpower in the United States, numbering 230 physicians per 100,000 population as opposed to 118 physicians in Britain, reflects a continuing theme of a two-to-one ratio of medical surplus in the United States. The two-to-one ratio of US specialists compared to primary physicians contrasts with an inverse ratio in the United Kingdom where GPs outnumber specialists by the same ratio. Hospitals, smaller and lavishly equipped in the United States, supply 390 beds per 100,000 population in the United States compared to 160 beds in the United Kingdom. The surfeit of personnel and capital assets translates into utilization; 40 million surgeries were performed on Americans in 1996, more than double the rate in Britain, with 3.5 million operations. Ninety million Americans visited the emergency room in 1996, twice as frequently as Britons, who clocked 11 million visits.

With twice the number of doctors performing twice the number of surgeries, do Americans live twice as long? Obviously not. Life expectancy is actually lower (seventy-six years in the United States compared to seventy-seven years in the United Kingdom). Looking closer at mortality data, a different tale unfolds. The four most frequent causes of death are the same on both sides of the Atlantic: ischemic heart disease (heart attack), carcinoma (cancer), cerebrovascular accidents (stroke), and COPD (bronchitis and emphysema). In all categories, Britain leads in mortality ratings: Deaths from acute myocardial infarction in the United Kingdom are 50 percent higher than the United States, cancer deaths are almost double the rate in Britain, and stroke three to four times higher.

Some deaths can be prevented; some cannot. The three leading causes of death, which can be prevented by modern health care, include ischemic heart disease, carcinoma of the breast, and colorectal carcinoma. Comparing mortality data for these conditions in the United States and the United Kingdom provides some consolation for the high-spending, fast-turnover medical practice in the United States. In 1996, over 2.5 million coronary angiograms were performed in the United States, less than 45,000 in the United Kingdom, an almost tenfold difference in utilization. Similarly, coronary artery bypass grafts were six times more common in the United States (598,000 in the United States, 20,000 in the United Kingdom). This massive investment pays off during an acute myocardial infarction, when an American's chance of survival is 50 percent higher than a Britain's.

Deaths from breast cancer, almost twice the rate in the United Kingdom, reflect the wide differential between mammography rates, the United States performing five times the per capita rate of screening mammograms. Deaths from colorectal cancer are almost double the rate in the United Kingdom, a statistic that is hard to separate from the fivefold greater rate of colonoscopy in the United States. The list goes on.

It is easy to calculate and account for the threefold greater cost of health care in the United States. Reassuringly, real impacts on some "preventable" diseases can be demonstrated in the United States, but at tremendous financial cost. As the baby boomers enter retirement age, those costs will only increase, with the added impact of fewer wage earners left to foot the bill.

In the United States, delegating decision making and rationing to third parties, such as HMOs, has proved flawed and irreconcilable. Alternative plans of rationalizing health consumption are proposed in schemes such as the Medical Savings Accounts, where difficult financial decisions are left to patients and their families. Although such schemes make sense to high-income earners (and Republicans), the American public is understandably reluctant to play guinea pig to another flawless scheme handed down from the great and good. Ironically the comprehensive failure of the HMO experiment moved America closer to a national health service, where dissatisfaction can not only be voiced but also voted.

In Britain, the NHS is certainly cost-effective for the national budget, but as a service industry, it remains chronically cash-strapped and overburdened. First priority is given to emergencies and acute life-threatening conditions. Whatever is left may be shared out thinly between elective, non-life-threatening conditions. Not all Britons' health needs can be satisfied, and those who are denied will continue to find their names either on a waiting list or a marble gravestone. Ironically, on the Appointed Day in 1948, the state assimilated the entire private health system, together with its capital and cash assets; a half century later an emerging private system now props up a struggling NHS.

The financial meltdown in the United States in 2008 produced a disaster comparable to Britain's wartime contraction. As the housing sector imploded, unemployment shot over 10 percent, the Dow lost in excess of 30 percent of its value, and the estimated cost of credit default swaps breached $62 trillion, the United States made the same left shift that Britain did in 1945. A single "public option" payer health care system was avoided by a handful of votes in the US Senate as the Affordable Care Act emerged. Of the original twenty-three state co-operatives set up under the Affordable Care Act, sixteen have been closed by state insurance regulators, after accumulating $1.7 billion dollar losses, and more in the pipeline, of the $2.4 billion dollar "loan" to set up the co-ops. Each of the remaining seven co-ops are operating in deficit, and plan double-digit rate increases to avoid closure.

Constrained by the new regulatory and administrative limitations in the act, the last men standing in the private health insurance industry are heading to the same insurance "death spiral" as Lehman, AIG, GM, and Chrysler. As soon as the last vestiges of the free market health insurers become wards of the US taxpayer, health care will devolve into the only logical solution—a single-payer US national health service, with all its second rate outcomes.

Why should the courts get into this messy business when Congress has designed a scheme to pay for itself?

—Justice Sandra Day O'Connor,
US Supreme Court Washington, DC.

Difficult and agonizing decisions have to be made as to how a limited budget is best allocated. ... That is not a judgment the court can make.

—Sir Thomas Bingham, Master of the Rolls
The Courts of Appeal, London.

Chapter 1

THE DEATH PANEL

AUTUMN 1981. SO HERE I WAS, TWENTY-FOUR YEARS OLD, a very recent graduate of Manchester Medical School, starting my first house job on the busy and prestigious renal dialysis unit of Manchester Royal Infirmary, one of the most prestigious hospitals in Britain and one of the largest teaching hospitals in Europe. Out of the blue, I was summoned from my daily tasks to a conference room to discuss the fate of Arthur, a thirty-five-year-old black male and an all-too-frequent flyer in the renal unit. I was not even sure why I had been summoned. I was a neophyte in medicine, even life, and a newcomer to the dialysis unit. The conference room was a bare utilitarian affair with a central wooden table and a worn, gray linoleum floor, surrounded by a handful of faded varnished wooden chairs, the seats worn bare by generations of incumbents. There were five people present. The consultant (the most senior rank in the NHS), a senior registrar (an upper rank in the myriad hierarchy of NHS), myself, and two social workers, whose presence I considered more questionable than even mine.

Arthur had presented something of a problem in the renal unit. He had been discharged and readmitted on multiple occasions in the last few months; he was noncompliant with his hypertension medications and had poorly controlled brittle diabetes from failure to take his insulin regularly. He required renal dialysis three times a week via a surgically placed dialysis catheter, which became infected on a regular basis and thrombosed (blocked by blood clots) because he failed to show up for his scheduled appointments for its heparinization. There was seemingly no end in sight for Arthur. His eligibility for long-term dialysis was doubtful. Resources were scarce in the dialysis unit, and as in any dialysis unit in Britain, renal dialysis machines were limited, personnel were stretched, and resources were thin. Arthur was unemployed, had no family, and his living circumstances, according to the social workers, were questionable, at best.

Arthur's eligibility and suitability for long-term dialysis using a surgically created arteriovenous fistula was the subject of the conference. Could or should we invest the scarce resources to create the arteriovenous fistula in his forearm, to enable dialysis three times a week to avert death from renal failure? Could he be trusted to follow up with his dialysis appointments in the years to come? If he did, and in the unlikely scenario that he did follow the rules, and on the vanishingly small chance that he qualified for the transplant list, would he be able or willing to manage his hypertension and diabetes after transplant to prevent a precious transplanted kidney from succumbing to the same fate as his own kidneys had suffered? This was not a judgment as to his merits to be placed on the renal transplant list, a much more deserving fate than chronic dialysis. This was about his qualifying for dialysis. Renal transplant had been performed for about twenty years, a relatively established procedure for the day, but renal transplants were still infrequent in the 1980s in Britain. Qualification for renal transplant was infinitely more demanding than dialysis. To get on the transplant list, patients had to be young, productive, compliant, and with the potential for a useful and productive life.

After medical school, I had landed my first choice of house jobs in the dialysis unit, demanding as it may be. At that time in Britain, medical school graduates were required to fulfill one year of in hospital "house jobs," or internships, prior to being certified by the BMA. Having completed the one year, newly fledged physicians were free to pursue whatever field they desired. For the fledgling house man (cynically referred to as the "housedog" among its own ranks), there was no ancillary staff, and it was the houseman's responsibility to perform all the menial, mundane, repetitive, and quasi-secretarial tasks required to keep the unit running smoothly. This also included nocturnal and emergency procedures, whatever the time of day or night, and whatever the circumstances. This was decades before any EU regulation of duty hours or the equivalent US ACGME restriction on trainee doctor's duty hours. There were no rules about maximum hours worked. The day started at 5:00 a.m. by filling out a pile of lab requests for electrolytes and hemoglobin levels. This is followed by drawing blood and sending it off to the lab for analysis, tabulating the results, and morning rounds at eight o'clock. Lab results were critical for morning rounds so that life-saving decisions could be made: dialysis or no dialysis; reduce life-threatening potassium levels; transfuse blood to maintain oxygenation and vital organ perfusion; infuse antirejection medications (cyclosporine, or shock doses of intravenous steroids) to avert kidney transplant rejection;

intravenous antibiotics for sepsis from dialysis catheters; or, in the event a donor kidney became available, screen potential recipients for blood- and tissue-type compatibility, get them into hospital, and screen them for surgery for a life-changing kidney transplant. Meanwhile, the clock ticked away on the viability of the donor kidney. For the houseman, there was no clock. There was a fog of night and day, of dark and light, of sleep and no sleep, of tasks done and not yet done.

In spite of their importance, the tasks were mundane, often grueling, mind-numbing, and repetitive. The patients in the renal unit were universally critically sick from fluid overload, electrolyte imbalance, and all the consequences of renal failure, which were many and potentially life-threatening. After a grueling day, it was routine to be called several times during the night to restart IV access, to perform and interpret EKGs for patients with chest pain or shortness of breath, to administer intravenous diazepam for patients with seizures, to infuse massive doses of Lasix for fluid overload, and most infuriating of all, because of its crass inefficiency (nurses were more than capable of performing this task), to inject heparin into the dialysis catheters of dialysis patients every four hours, around the clock, to prevent them becoming occluded from clot formation. Sleep deprivation was the norm. In the small hours of one fateful night, a fellow houseman on the same unit as me erroneously injected a vial of epinephrine into a patient's dialysis catheter, mistaking it for the anticoagulant Heparin. In his exhausted and sleep-deprived mind, in the semidark of the small hours of the morning, in the dimmed light, he was unable to clearly read the label of the vial he was about to inject. The patient had an immediate cardiac arrest at the end of the syringe. As any houseman or intern will attest, my days were filled with numbing exhaustion with intermittent sleep characterized, in my particular case, by the aura of flashing lights in my sleep-drenched mind and involuntary twitching of my limbs, as I fell into a deep sleep prior to the telephone ringing yet again to perform another routine, mundane task. Chronic exhaustion entails a permanent feeling of nausea, overwhelming fatigue, and a zombie- or fugue-like state. This was Sleep Deprivation 101. It is currently, in the post-9/11 world, a favorite form of torture.

The renal unit was located at the polar opposite corner of Manchester Royal Infirmary (MRI) from the doctor's dormitory where the housemen lived, slept, and ate during the first year of their careers. Manchester Royal Infirmary was a huge, expansive building built in 1908, a very recent addition to the National Health Service. Summoned to the renal unit during the night involved rolling out of bed, typically fully dressed from flopping exhausted into bed, and trudging the cavernous halls to the renal unit. Nearby, a local Manchester hospital, Withington Hospital, built in 1728, the elder statesman of Greater Manchester NHS, boasted a houseman's nighttime bicycle that he or she could ride down the quarter-mile hospital corridor, perform this task, and return to the doctors' dormitory by the same means. At MRI, we had no such luxury. I showered infrequently, ate when I could, and slept wherever and whenever the opportunity presented itself.

Arthur was a frequent flyer in the renal unit, and this presented a problem. He had frequent admissions with fluid overload due to noncompliance with fluid restrictions, pneumonia from heavy smoking, and failure to maintain a low-protein diet. Not much of a life, for most people. His dialysis catheter became frequently infected, requiring frequent changes. So a decision had to be made: thumbs-up or thumbs-down. Given the limited resources available, difficult choices had to be made. Nonetheless, I did not wish to be part of that process.

Born on a hardscrabble sheep farm in north Yorkshire, I was accustomed to hard work and making do. I'd arrived in medicine as a second choice of career. Located in the middle of the north Yorkshire moors, the farm was a derelict collection of a half-dozen buildings and a limestone farmhouse. It showed every bit of its more than hundred years. From an early age, my sister and I milked cows, sheared sheep, cut acres of grass, baled hay, and picked and planted potatoes. We learned to drive tractors at a very early age. Moorland soil is no environment to grow crops other than heather, gorse bushes, scraggly grass, and a few stunted potatoes. Moorland soil is very acidic and contains lots of iron, manifested by the rust-brown deposits of iron oxide in the beds of moorland streams.

Compared to the more fertile soils in the vale of York, twenty miles south, our farm was a moorland moonscape. My father, the youngest of ten children, acquired the less-than-desirable farm since it was the most affordable available at the time. The youngest child got the leftovers. He would spend the remainder of his unexpectedly short life trying to convert the unforgiving moorland to arable land.

Although the youngest of ten siblings, he would be the first to die. Trying to make the land productive entailed plowing the heather-strewn earth, revealing a heavy crop of rocks and stones. It was my and my sister's job to pick up the rocks and stones in the wake of the plow and throw them manually onto a trailer in the wake of the plow. The first step to tilling the soil was to make it arable. The worn-out tractor was an ancient

Massey Ferguson. My sister and I put the tractor into first gear and "low" box, set the throttle at crawl speed, and let the tractor idle unmanned down the plow furrows. Thereupon, we would jump off the slow-moving tractor and manually claw and dig the rocks out of the tilled earth and throw them onto the equally ancient flatbed trailer that it pulled behind. Reaching the end of the furrow, we would nimbly climb on the back of the tractor to avoid being crushed by its massive wheels, turn it around, and point it down the next furrow to repeat the process. It was very obvious that the most reliable crop that the farm would ever produce would be rocks and stones.

In the summer, the Yorkshire dales are a beautiful, undulating tranquil ocean of green fields, ancient dry stone walls, and purple seas of heather, attracting weekend visitors driving through the country lanes. In winter, the frozen rain and snow are whipped and blown horizontally by the gusting winds. The farmhouse, over a century old, had no central heating and an unreliable water source from a well located in a nearby field. The water filter was a wad of chicken wire, which trapped the larger animals that fell into the well. In the winter, I would scratch the frost from the inside of my bedroom window to see what the weather was doing outside. Not a very optimistic predictor of the conditions outside.

Growing up on a barren farm in northern England in pre-Thatcher Britain, I had an early introduction to the prevailing Labor government's socialist ways. As part of Britain's post–World War II socialist overhaul, the Ministry of Agriculture was created to control every facet of Britain's farming sector. It was unlawful for us to sell the milk from our cows, the wool from the sheep, or even the beef cattle on the private market. The milk had to be "sold" to the Milk Marketing Board, the wool to the Wool Marketing Board, and the beef to the Hill Cow Board. In return for a bare-minimum guaranteed price, a subsidy check would arrive once a month to "make up the difference" from market prices. Were it not so tragic, the whole system will be laughable. Having opened a subsidy check from the Milk Marketing Board one day, my father's shoulders sagged as he placed the check on the kitchen table. I looked at the check, and the amount paid was less than the stamp on the envelope in which it had arrived. The work was hard, grueling, and unrewarding. I wasn't sure what I was going to do with my life, but I wasn't going to be no sheep farmer.

Growing up on an isolated farm, my sister and I learned quickly about the delicate balance between life and death. In the spring, we delivered lambs when the sheep were too exhausted to deliver them by themselves. Having smaller hands than my father, we were instructed to put our hands in the birth canal of the sheep, feel for the lamb's hooves, and pull the lamb from the exhausted sheep. The best way to resuscitate an unresponsive lamb was to place baler twine, a brittle hemp rope used to tie hay and straw bales, into the lamb's nostril. This invariably produced a forceful expulsion of the amniotic fluid from the lamb's lungs, which typically would then revive. Many times, we were too late, and both ewe and lamb died an unimaginable death from exhaustion. Even if the sheep managed to deliver a live lamb, the newborn lamb was always prey for ever-present carrion crows, which would swoop out of the sky and peck out the living lamb's eyes, leaving it to die, killing it slowly for a later feast. During lambing season, we always walked the fields and moors armed with a rifle to wade off constant threats from predators: crows, stray dogs, foxes.

Difficult labor for cows was more complex. On several occasions, in order to assist the exhausted cow, we would place ropes on the protruding forelegs of the obstructed calf, and my father, mother, sister, and I would pull with all our strength in an attempt to pull the lamb from the exhausted cow. If this failed, the rope was tied to the tow bar of a tractor. In first gear, we would pull the tractor very gently forward, so releasing the calf from the exhausted cow. As brutal as it sounds, this saved many animals in the course of our upbringing. The vet was called only as the very last resort. A dead cow or sheep is worth nothing, and if there were no prospects for survival, the animal was dispatched at the end of a rifle. If there was some prospect of a more viable cow, calf, horse, or foal, the vet was summoned.

One of the local vets was none other than James Herriot, a famous author of many novels such as *All Creatures Great and Small*, *If Only They Could Talk*, and *All Things Bright and Beautiful*. His real name was James Wight, and his practice was located in nearby Thirsk. He wrote of the local dales, the grueling but fascinating farm life, and the colorful farmers, make for best-selling reads. His blockbuster novels converted to movies and TV series. Having called for the vet for a stricken animal, I would watch them pull into the pothole-ridden farmyard in their well-equipped Land Rovers, retrieve the appropriate instruments from a neat array of stainless steel trays in the vehicle's rear compartment, and stride confidently to their task. I knew exactly what I wanted to do in life: I wanted to be a veterinary surgeon. I wanted to be James Herriot.

Over the years, I would assist the vets during their visits to the farm as they performed cesarean sections on horses, castrated steers, and performed surgery on gastric volvulus in cows. They were my heroes. On one occasion we were in a tiny stable with an almost fully grown horse, about to perform a castration. Unfortunately, my father was a consummate procrastinator, leaving procedures to be performed on almost fully grown animals rather than months earlier. This made the procedure infinitely more difficult and dangerous. The horse's head was tied to the hayrick; the newly graduated, and obviously inexperienced vet inserted an IV into the horse's neck and injected a potent sedative to anesthetize the horse. As the horse's eyes began to close, we moved to the horse's rear (a very dangerous place, as I well knew) to perform surgery. As he carefully placed the scalpel on the horse's scrotum, the horse reared, bucked wildly, flailing his rear legs in the tiny stable, and broke loose from his tether. As the horse bucked wildly out of control, somehow we both flew into the safety of the hayrick as the horse continued to buck, squeal, and rear. As my father opened the stable door to see what the commotion was about, the horse bolted from the stable. To this day, I'm not sure how we both managed to escape that incident with our lives, which almost ended a promising career for him and almost ended mine before it had started.

Announcing to my father I planned to go to veterinary school, he shook his head, moaning that their bills were too high and their businesses would soon fail. Reluctantly listening to his advice, I chose my second option and applied to medical school.

I excelled at the local Ripon High School and was lucky enough to be accepted at the age of eighteen to my first choice of medical schools, in Manchester. The subsequent five years were filled with hundreds of lectures, late-night studying, and scores of mind-racking exams. For entertainment, my three medical school roommates and I played rugby and soccer and drank beer. During vacations, I returned to the farm to help pick potatoes, make hay, lead straw and milk cows, and shear sheep. If I was lucky, I landed a job on a local construction site, which actually produced a paycheck, the first in my life. After five years of medical school, and having successfully graduated as a full-fledged doctor, I landed my first house job in the prestigious dialysis unit of Manchester Royal Infirmary. Located immediately next door to the medical school, I had landed one of the most prestigious and sought-after house jobs available. I was thrilled.

Dialysis patients are exceedingly complex management problems due to the profound impact of a nonfunctioning renal system. They become fluid overloaded very rapidly, and they must adhere strictly to a special diet avoiding protein, which is excreted by the kidney; they develop life-threatening electrolyte disturbances, which can result in cessation of the heart or rapid arrhythmias. These were long, grueling days with equally long, sleep-deprived nights. Hard as it was, it was certainly better than the farm.

One day I found myself being summoned to the conference room, taken away from my myriad outstanding tasks and responsibilities of drawing labs, collecting results, admitting patients in renal failure, and the endless other tasks assigned to the houseman. The topic of the meeting was the future of Arthur. Arthur's prospects for long-term dialysis, and therefore of life itself, were grim. Because of the limited resources and scarce funding, it was necessary to decide who was more eligible for dialysis, leaving the less eligible ones to die. Arthur had been dealt a poor hand in life's game of poker, and he did not make the cut. This meant that no more dialysis would be performed, and he would be left to die from renal failure. Nobody wanted to be there. Nobody wanted to make these decisions, but there were no other options. It was a thumbs-down.

Having very little experience in my chosen career of medicine, I was disgusted but mostly sad for Arthur, who I had grown close to during the long days and nights of managing his renal failure. In retrospect, the decision was predictable and predetermined.

As usual the following morning, I drew blood from the patients, including Arthur, collected the reports, and interpreted the results. His BUN and creatinine were sky high, his white cell count had shot through the roof, he had a massive left shift, probably from overwhelming pneumonia, his glucose was off the chart, and there was not a single normal laboratory parameter. He had multisystem organ failure, and he had hours to live.

We performed rounds dutifully at eight o'clock and stood at the foot of Arthur's bed. "How is he?" I shook my head. We passed on in silence. Later that evening, I went back to Arthur's bedside before turning in for the night. As a result of renal failure, his breath was foul, smelling of urine, and he drifted in and out of consciousness. His breathing was heavy but sporadic and irregular—Cheynes-Stokes breathing, a sign of imminent death. His lungs still attempted to blow off the accumulated acid from this renal failure in the form of exhaled carbon dioxide, so-called "air hunger," but in vain. I gently ran my fingernails down his forearm, and in their wake, a track of what appeared to be a white frost traced from his black skin. Tiny crystals of urea, accumulated in his skin, created a shimmering track known as uremic frost. I had read about uremic frost, but I had never seen this before and never cared to see it again. Still, I remember it as if it were yesterday. A few hours later, at 3:00 a.m., I was summoned by the night nurse to the renal unit to pronounce Arthur dead. His pupils were fixed and dilated, and his heavy jowl sagged lifelessly. I listen to his heart and lungs. Nothing. I wrote, as I would do for the next twenty to thirty years when a patient would die from the hands of Mother Nature or from what I could have done or could not have done, "Deceased, RIP" This was my first experience of rationing and its consequences. There would be many more.

Chapter 2

THE FIVE GIANTS

IN 1900, QUEEN VICTORIA HAD BEEN ON THE THRONE FOR fifty-three years and ruled an empire incorporating 20 percent of the globe. The British Empire boasted over 450 million subjects, one-quarter of the world's population. Britain controlled 20 percent of world trade, and her ships transported 45 percent of the world's maritime cargo. Seventy-five percent of world trade was financed through the Bank of England. In spite of Britain's preeminence as the world's only superpower, the Victorians reserved some of its harshest treatment for their own citizens at home. However, the turn of the century brought reappraisal of social conditions in Britain and a reevaluation of the Victorian values of self-dependence and intolerance of poverty. A series of inquiries into social conditions were commissioned, the most important by Seebohm Rowntree, founder of the York-based chocolate empire. In 1901, Rowntree reported that one-third of the population of the city of York was living in poverty, a figure that prevailed throughout Britain. The Victorians had tolerated the suffering in their midst, and even the Tory governments of the late 1800s had recognized that an industrial economy had relied on "an enormous mass of paupers" as a labor force to maintain its momentum. The turn of the century brought a new look at poverty, and the "impotent poor" of the Victorian era became the "deserving poor" of the new Edwardian age. "The problem of 1834 was a problem of pauperism, the problem of 1893 is a problem of poverty," remarked Alfred Marshall, a leading economist of the time.

The great liberal reformer David Lloyd George set in motion the political machinery for welfare reform in Britain in the first decades of the 1900s. The man who drew up the blueprint for the welfare state designed each of its parts, and put the whole together as a fully functional system was William Henry Beveridge.

William Beveridge, born in 1879 in India, the son of a judge in the civil service, was sent back home to be educated at Oxford University. Having obtained his law degree, he spent time teaching and writing newspaper articles before being given his big break in 1908 when he joined the Board of Trade as a civil servant under the liberal government of Herbert Asquith. In the Board of Trade, he would develop a lifelong relationship with the then-liberal MP and newly appointed president of the Board of Trade, Winston Churchill. At the time, Winston Churchill was a liberal-minded reformer with much ideology in common with Beveridge; however, Churchill's political ideology would shift rightward over the course of the decades as he abandoned the idealistic beliefs of his youth. At the time, however, Winston Churchill and Lloyd George were swept along on a tidal wave of post-Victorian reforms, intent on bettering the lot of the common man. The two political figureheads, referred to as the "Heavenly Twins" because of their common ideology, were each destined to lead Britain through a world war: Lloyd George, as prime minister from 1915 to 1918, and Winston Churchill from 1939 to 1945. Although Beveridge and Churchill's relationship would be lifelong, Churchill's rightward political drift would lead him to see Beveridge's plans in a different light in 1942, when he published the Beveridge Report on welfare reform. "An awful windbag, and a dreamer" was one of Churchill's less flattering remarks about Beveridge's plans for a post–World War II Britain.

Lloyd George became prime minister in 1915 and led Britain during the war years of World War I, while Winston Churchill rose through a series of ministerial offices culminating in his appointment as First Lord of the Admiralty at the outset of World War I. Churchill's political career floundered in 1915 as a result of his proposing the ill-fated Dardanelles Campaign. In 1915, the trenches stretched from the Channel Coast to the Swiss Alps in an unassailable, unbroken line. Winston Churchill, as First Lord of the Admiralty, spearheaded a plan to send a large British naval force into the Eastern Mediterranean, and land in the lightly defended southern flank of the Axis Powers on the Dardanelles peninsula. The plan called for a naval strike through the narrow Bosporus Straits into the Black Sea, where the naval guns could strike Constantinople and the soft Turkish underbelly. Because of hesitation on the part of the fleet commanders, however, the landings were delayed long enough for the Turks to assemble a sufficient force to counter the landings and result in a bloody stalemate, which would result in 250,000 Australian and New Zealand casualties. Winston Churchill became the scapegoat for the fiasco. "I am the victim of a political intrigue. I am finished," he confided in a friend. Believing his political life was over, he left his post in the admiralty to join an infantry regiment in France for the most of the remainder of the war.

Although Churchill's political career eventually overcame the legacy of the Dardanelles campaign, the events were remembered all too clearly by the voting public during the 1945 general election. As World War II entered its closing stages, a still bellicose Churchill called on the British public to take up arms against yet another enemy, this time, the Soviet Union. Drained by war and weary of conflict, the voters dismissed Winston Churchill by a decisive margin at the polls. This unexpected (even to the victors) turn of events ushered in one of the most radical left-wing British governments of the twentieth century, so setting the stage for radical reforms, including a National Health Service.

With his wartime defeats behind him, Winston Churchill would leave the liberal party in 1924 and rejoin the conservative ranks as MP for Epping that same year. Appointed Chancellor of the Exchequer shortly afterward, he would attract public attention for his role in breaking the general strike in 1926, an action that would place him in the ranks opposing his future political adversary, Aneurin Bevan. Bevan, a radical left-wing organizer of the Welsh mining unions, had risen through the ranks of the Welsh mining unions to become Labor MP and vocal critic of Churchill's wartime coalition government. His future role as minister of health in the post–World War II Labor government would make him the central figure in shaping Britain's health service.

From 1929 to 1939, Churchill would be without ministerial office but remained a vocal critic of Chamberlain's appeasement policies toward Hitler and Mussolini. For ten years he would remain a rebel conservative backbencher, accurately predicting Hitler and Mussolini's next moves, and berating the Chamberlain government for their lack of action and unpreparedness for war. As a maverick backbencher, Churchill's strident anti-Nazi rhetoric in the 1930s would make him a political figurehead in his own right. He had maintained close contacts in all key areas relating to Britain's readiness for war and on the maneuvering of Nazi Germany in Europe in the late 1930s.

Much of Churchill's information was delivered by his informers to his country home in Chartwell or his London flat at Morpeth Mansions. A steady stream of visitors and dinner guests would leave packages of critical and top secret information regarding the war situation on the dining room table, which Churchill would digest and later divulge to Parliament. Churchill's clandestine informants, whom he himself described as "special sources of intelligence," included three cabinet ministers and several high-ranking officers from the army, navy, and air force. Sir Eustace Tennyson d'Eyncourt supplied classified information regarding the balance of naval power. Charles Anderson, director of training for the Air Ministry, supplied up-to-date and accurate data regarding the readiness of the Royal Air Force. Ralph Wigram, head of the Foreign Office "central department," supplied data on Germany's war preparations. Desmond Morton, chief of the industrial intelligence unit of the "Committee of Imperial Defense," provided classified information regarding Germany's arms buildup. Lachlan Maclean, senior air staff officer for bomber command, supplied data on offensive capabilities of the bomber squadrons.

Among these dinner guests leaving, in turn, his brown manila envelope was William, Beveridge, then working in the Manpower Services Commission and possessing detailed statistics on manpower availability in the event of war. This clandestine network of anti-Chamberlain government informers delivering packets of top secret information to the dinner table seems almost comical in retrospect. Nonetheless, at the time, the stakes for Britain and the personalities involved were never higher, and leakage of classified material could certainly have landed the perpetrators in jail, or worse. It is to Beveridge's credit that he placed himself among those willing to run the risk of imprisonment or even death, acts that would give him greater credibility in the years to come, and place him on the right side of history. As a result of this intelligence, Parliament listened to Churchill's detailed accounts of the government's own discounted information with increasing disquiet. His monologues were greeted first with ridicule, then unease, and finally, as Hitler's intentions became clear to all, with alarm.

At the outbreak of war, his accurate predictions of the Axis intentions and clarion call to arms earned him his old post as First Lord of the Admiralty. In May 1940, when Chamberlain's appeasement policies forced him to resign, Churchill was swept to power as leader of a coalition government by a unanimous vote of 380–0, faced with the task of reversing Britain's so-far-disastrous involvement in the war.

In July 1940, Beveridge was appointed to an almost bureaucratic backwater entitled the Interdepartmental Committee on Social Security and Allied Services. His brief was to streamline the patchwork of social security systems dating from the Victorian Poor Law and later Edwardian legislation.

Beveridge found a fragmented and tangled system of social security benefits, including unemployment insurance; national health insurance; old-age pensions; and widows', orphans', and war victims' benefits paid by a polyglot of departments in unrelated ministries. Huge gaps existed in benefit provision, many programs were duplicated, and inequities abounded. Beveridge developed the concept of a single national insurance administered by a single department that provided universal coverage. Beveridge popularized his plan for universal benefits by describing five giants that stood in the way of prosperity and health for the whole nation. These giants, which he enumerated as "Want," "Idleness," "Disease," "Squalor," and "Ignorance," would be attacked individually and collectively by separate acts of legislation that would be passed over the course of the next decade. "Want" was attacked by the expansion of the national health insurance scheme, providing universal benefits for all workers in the event of sickness, disease, or disability. "Squalor" would be addressed by the Housing Act of 1948, which was responsible for rebuilding the million homes destroyed and three million damaged in the war years, replacing them in a massive state building project. The red-brick, semidetached council house estates, the result of the rebuilding program, still dot the British urban landscape. "Ignorance" would be attacked by increasing the school leaving age to a minimum of fifteen years of age, a provision embodied in the Education Act of 1946. "Disease" would be countered by comprehensive and universal coverage for every citizen, provided by the state, and free at the point of consumption; this would see the light of day as the National Health Service Act of 1948, the most all-encompassing and enduring of Beveridge's proposals. The fifth giant, "Idleness," would prove more difficult in practice to slay, although the provision of full employment was a somewhat superficial answer provided in the report.

The provision of universal social security and health care was only one side of the coin. The second, in Beveridge's words, was "first and foremost a method of redistributing income and to make the best possible use of whatever sources are available." Having said that, Beveridge was careful to point out that he did not want the state "to stifle initiative, opportunity, or responsibility." His objectives, he maintained, were to benefit the circumstances of the individual rather than extending the power of the state. A clearer picture of Beveridge's intentions in his report was illustrated by a report in the conservative *Daily Telegraph* when he boasted his report would "take us halfway to Moscow," a statement that was followed by a mild disclaimer shortly afterward. The report, with the bland title of "Social Insurance and Allied Services," was expected to be published between September and November 1942. Delays in publishing the report until December 1942 resulted in an unexpected and unanticipated public relations boom.

In the three years of war prior to the release of the Beveridge Report, Britons were starved of good news. From whatever theater of war they cared to look, the news was grim, with almost daily reports of retreats, surrenders, and setbacks. The situation was most critical at home. Britain, an island nation, had been isolated since 1939 when the German forces rolled through Europe to the continental coasts. Britain relied almost entirely on imports of raw materials in order to pursue the war, even for basic foodstuffs that could not be grown at home. In the previous year, 1941, sixty million tons of imports had reached Britain. In 1942, this figure dropped to thirty-three million, a direct result of U-boat sinkings of cargo vessels in the North Atlantic. The loss of cargo shipping compounded the problem and magnified the losses. With limited raw materials, the British shipyards could not produce transports in sufficient number or rapidly enough to replace the losses. The break-even point for Britain lay at eight hundred thousand tons of shipping a month. Losses in excess of this number could not be replaced at a sufficient rate, and Britain entered a deficit mode. If these losses continued, Britain would slowly starve to death and be unable to pursue the war. In a single week in July 1941, nearly four hundred thousand tons of shipping had been lost, more than twice the limited of sustainable loss. In a single week in November, losses increased to 721,000 tons of shipping, a rate of four times the break point. Britain was on the brink of starvation and paralysis.

In the Far East, Britain suffered defeat after defeat. Hong Kong surrendered to the Japanese in December 1941, followed in short order by the loss of two capital ships, *The Prince of Wales* and *Repulse*, both sunk by Japanese torpedo planes. On February 14, 1942, Singapore, Britain's foothold in the Far East, surrendered to the Japanese after a five-day siege, with a loss of sixty-two thousand Allied soldiers to Japanese prisoner of war camps.

In North Africa, Tobruk, the gateway to Cairo and Suez Canal, fell to the Africa Corp with a loss of 33,000 allied soldiers. The road to Cairo, the Suez Canal, and the oil fields of the Middle East was wide open. In the Russian theater, a series of convoys transporting munitions to Murmansk were mauled with considerable loss of shipping, munitions, and life. In April 1942, an Arctic convoy, PQ17, consisting of thirty-four ships, was severely mauled by German U-boats, with the loss of twenty-three of their number. Of the surviving eleven ships, only four entered the harbor at Murmansk to offload its munitions, the remaining ships scattering to find shelter in the archipelagos off Northern Russia. So devastating were the losses that the convoys scheduled for August and September were canceled. In November 1942, PQ19, consisting of forty ships, suffered a similar fate at the hands of the U-boats, losing thirteen ships in the Arctic Circle. In the fall of 1942, the question on most Britons' minds was not if there would be a British welfare state, but whether there would be a British state at all.

Nonetheless, Beveridge continued through the dark months of 1940 to 1942 to plan for his welfare state. In October 1942, at which time Beveridge's report was widely expected, Montgomery launched his attack on the Axis forces at El Alamein in North Africa. From October 23, 1942, through the next two and a half weeks, the battle raged, but this time, the Allies prevailed, pushing Rommel and the Africa Corps back into the Libyan Desert. This was the first good news in three and a half years.

In November, Operation Torch landed US Forces in Algiers, in the rear of Rommel's Africa Corp, which would be trapped between the two Allied forces and forced to surrender several months later. Britons breathed a collective sigh of relief, and for the first time in many years, they allowed themselves to ponder a postwar Britain. "Let the church bells ring all over England," boomed Churchill, to celebrate Montgomery's victory at El Alamein. Hardly had the bells ceased to toll when Beveridge presented his long-awaited plan to an eager public. The timing of the release of Beveridge's report could not have been stage-managed more perfectly to be received by a public, so recently delivered from the jaws of defeat.

Britain was in the mood for a large act of collectiveness and union. This is precisely what Beveridge had in mind. The report was released to the general public on December 19, 1942. The report had been widely anticipated in the months leading to its final release. Even members of Parliament raised questions in the House of Commons about the expected date of release. Parts of the report had been leaked to the press; the BBC had even broadcast excerpts in the weeks leading to its release. Special interest groups had prepared defenses and attempted to sabotage the report prior to its release and subsequent parliamentary debate. Within two weeks of publication, Gallop Poll reported nineteen out of twenty people had heard of the report, and nine out of ten believed it should be adopted. Thousands lined up outside His Majesty's stationary office to buy a copy of the report, of which six hundred fifty thousand were sold, making it the war's most unlikely best seller.

Parliamentary debate on the report opened on February 16, 1943. The government of the day accepted the report in broad principle, although expressing reservations about the cost of the plan, especially those for a National Health Service. "Generous hearts do not foot bills," explained the chancellor of the exchequer, Sir Kingsley Wood. There was strong support from the Labor benches, especially for the planned National Health Service. "State medical services should be expanded and brought within the reach of a wider public," expounded the Labor shadow minister of health. Labor leader and deputy prime minister in the coalition government, Clement Attlee, who was to become prime minister after World War II, greeted the plan unreservedly. So too did Aneurin Bevan, future minister of health in the postwar Labor government.

With an eye on reshaping post–World War II Britain, and with the possibility of forming the first Labor governments in fifteen years, Attlee and Bevan greeted the promise of the new social order enthusiastically and promised the war-weary British public a brave new world, "a new Jerusalem." The Labor

Party had interpreted the mood of the British public correctly and would be rewarded generously at the polls three years later in 1945. Churchill and the conservatives, while "greeting" the plan, paid little more than lip service to its proposals. Churchill could not fathom how the public could expect to "vote themselves a better standard of living," and besides, there were currently more serious threats to face. Churchill and the conservatives had misread the mood of the land, and they would pay dearly in the upcoming election.

Having accepted the plan in broad principle, the political groundwork had been laid for the planning and development of postwar National Health Service in some shape or form. A series of plans were floated by the coalition government's Ministry of Health. Meetings were held with the involved parties, the municipal hospitals, the voluntary hospitals, the general practitioners (GPs), and the specialist doctors. The first plan, the Brown Plan, proposed in March 1943, recommended utilizing the municipal hospitals as a centerpiece of the plan, which would be funded and run by local governments. The voluntary hospitals would participate but would not be nationalized. General practitioners would be employed full time by the local government. The British Medical Association was firm in their opposition. The GPs and specialists refused to become employees of local government, many of which were not up to the task of taking on such a large added responsibility. Besides, the specter of the old Poor Law still hung around the neck of the municipal hospitals.

February 1944 brought the first official white paper, "A National Health Service," composed by the new minister of health, Henry Willink. This plan recommended combining local authorities into area authorities that would finance and run the municipal hospitals within its jurisdiction. The voluntary hospitals would participate and be reimbursed in proportion to the services rendered. The GPs would be under contract with a central body, the Central Medical Board, but would be reimbursed by the prewar arrangement through the National Insurance Plan. By the summer of 1945, the plan had been amended to incorporate the wishes of several interested and aggrieved parties, producing a plan "of nightmarish complexity." By this time, the surrender of Germany was close at hand, and the prospects for a general election lay close. Plans for a future National Health Service would take a dramatic turn to the left under the new minister of health, the volatile and outspoken Aneurin Bevan.

With the surrender of Germany on May 8, 1945, the Labor Party leadership was anxious to dissolve the wartime coalition government, and call for a general election. Churchill wished to continue the coalition government until the final defeat of Japan. However, the prospects of a Labor victory and the formation of the first Labor government in almost fifteen years proved too much for the party faithful. At their annual meeting in Blackpool, on the northwest coast of England, the Labor Party executive voted to withdraw their support from the coalition government, dissolve Parliament, and call an early general election. Clement Attlee telephoned Winston Churchill on May 21 to deliver the bad news, and two days later, on May 23, Churchill went to Buckingham Palace and fulfilled his constitutional requirements to hand the seals of office to the king, dissolving the government. The general election was now underway. Churchill's principal campaign theme was the threat of a rising Soviet presence in Eastern Europe. As a secondary issue, he outlined his plans for implementing a watered-down version of the Beveridge plan, including the

National Health Service. He then returned to his central theme of controlling and expanding Soviet threat at the east.

Polling day was set for July 5, 1945, and the results were to be announced three weeks later, on July 26, the long delay being necessary to collect and count ballots from British servicemen scattered all over the world. Arrangements had already been made for a meeting of the "big three," Truman, Churchill, and Stalin, to be held in Potsdam on July 16, 1945. The purpose of the conference was to discuss the role of the victorious Allied powers throughout the world. Ten days after polling day, Winston Churchill traveled to Potsdam, with Clement Attlee in tow, because of the possibility, albeit unlikely in Churchill's eyes, that Attlee could have been voted in as prime minister on polling day. The discussions with Stalin proved to be contentious, and as Churchill expected, his plans for Soviet expansion in the world were clear to all. Nonetheless, during a private meeting between Churchill and Stalin, the Soviet leader confided in him that he expected that the conservatives would win easy reelection, with the majority of at least eighty seats in the new 585-member Parliament. Plans were made for Churchill and Attlee to fly back to Britain on the twenty-fifth, the day before the results were to be announced. On Churchill's departure from Potsdam, both Truman and Stalin expected to see him back forty-eight hours later to conclude the conference as the newly elected British prime minister. On returning to Britain on the evening of the July 25, a great despondency hung over the Labor Party headquarters, where an imminent electoral defeat was expected, with a projected shortfall of thirty seats.

The following morning, the first sign that all was not going well for the conservatives came by midmorning. By 10:00 a.m., ten conservative seats had already fallen to Labor. Churchill, at his home in Chartwell, was given the bad news by an aide. "The prime minister was in his bath," he recalled, "and he appeared surprised, if not shocked." By lunchtime, it was clear that the Labor Party had been elected by a landslide. The postwar election of 1945 was one of the greatest political upheavals in modern British political history. The British public and its armed forces, having fought the entire duration of the six-year war, were not interested in pursuing yet another crusade against the Soviets, nor did they wish to return home to endure a second postwar recession, as it happened after the First World War. Clement Attlee's promise of a "New Jerusalem," and Beveridge's plans for "cradle-to-grave benefits for all," sounded good to them. The Labor Party held an unassailable majority in the new Parliament, with 374 seats held by Labor to 150 seats by the conservatives. Churchill, having led Britain through a six-year war, was dismayed. His wife, Constance, suggested that the results may be a blessing in disguise. "It's a very good disguise," was the terse reply.

Clement Attlee's new Labor government acted quickly and decisively to implement the measures of the Beveridge plan. With a mandate for change and an unassailable majority in Parliament, the Labor Party set about its promised postwar reconstruction of Britain. However, the country faced the hard reality that although on the winning side of the war, it was no longer a major world power. Its cities had been bombed, one million homes destroyed and three million damaged. Its industrial base had been eroded; many of its overseas possessions had been lost for good or signed over as collateral for war debt.

The new government introduced and passed an unprecedented blizzard of legislation in Parliament during the first year. The Industrial Injuries Bill provided state-run disability insurance. An extended National Health Insurance guaranteed unemployment benefits and a pension scheme for all. School leaving age was increased to fifteen years of age, and plans were made for building over a million state-funded "council houses," named after local government's title of "county council." Rebuilding housing was a priority, and the New Tenements Bill of 1946 brought about the building of new communities outside the major cities in what had been, up until then, farmland. Thousands of brick, semidetached council houses, with a standard three bedrooms, living room, kitchen, and bathroom, were built by the state and rented by local government for a standard rent of a modest "sixteen shillings and sixpence." The greatest of these acts, however, was the National Health Service Act of 1946, providing everything from free medical, hospital and dental treatment for all, free at the point of consumption. The plan provided free dentures, spectacles, and wigs, provided by the state at no cost to the patient. The welfare state was up and running.

Attlee's new government faced monumental hurdles other than welfare provision in the postwar years: Britain was broke. After six years of war, the trade gap was a gaping chasm, and Britain's entire industrial infrastructure, that which remained, was entirely war related.

Britain's balance sheet was grim. In 1940, in order to continue the war, Churchill had negotiated the terms of Lend-Lease, whereby arms and munitions would be leased on a rental basis until the end of the war when payment would become due. On February 8, 1941, the House of Representatives had voted a $4.736 billion package by 260–165 votes. The Senate followed by a sixty to thirty-one majority one month later.

Britain had little leverage to negotiate: a considerable down payment was required, consisting of the balance of Britain's gold reserves (amounting to only $574 Million at the end of 1940) and Britain's commercial assets in the United States. "We are not to be skinned, but flayed to the bone," lamented Churchill privately to an aide. The original deal was for six months of supplies and expired in November 1941, when further sums were negotiable. Fortunately for the exchequer, the Japanese attack on Pearl Harbor was one month away.

Sustained by US imports to Britain during the war years, Lend-Lease was abruptly canceled by Truman one week after the surrender of the Japanese. Attlee's government had inherited a huge war debt, with little equity or assets to pay it off. Much of Britain's overseas assets, from rubber plantations to tin mines, had been signed over to US control under the terms of Lend-Lease. Others had been temporarily lost to the Axis powers, many of which, having been left to fend for themselves during the war, had independence in mind. To maintain basic necessities, to furnish its massive war debt, and to retain a credible armed force overseas against a possible Russian threat, Attlee asked for a further $5 billion loan from the United States. Britain secured a $4.375 billion loan, albeit at an interest rate of 2 percent and payable over fifty years. "Generous, by US standards," grumbled the new chancellor of the exchequer. Although emerging a victor from the war, Britain had to face the fact that she was no longer a global power and was bankrupt.

Relief came in the form of the Marshall Plan, a gift rather than a loan as was Lend-Lease. The four-year plan granted a total of $13.3 billion, 1.2 percent of the now-bloated US GDP, to be distributed among the warring European countries, to be spent as they felt best. Britain would receive the lion's share 24 percent of the total, France 21.2 percent, Italy 11.85 percent, and Germany 10.8 percent. France invested heavily in its transport infrastructure, principally railways. Britain's pet project was its new welfare state. Not only did this avert national insolvency and its social and political consequences, but also it made the introduction of the welfare state a reality.

Having secured financial backing for the new welfare state, Attlee's government embarked on a second great wave of postwar reconstruction involved incorporating entire industries under government ownership. The utilities—electricity, oil, gas, and water—were all each assimilated by the state. Communications—telephone, air transport, road, rail, and waterway transport—were all nationalized. The coal and steel industries (soon to prove the most militant of the new public sector industries) were assimilated under public ownership. Even the Bank of England, independent since before 1710, came under state control. By 1950, 20 percent of all British industry had been taken into public ownership. New names appeared on the British landscape: British Steel, British Gas, British Telecom, British Airways, and British Rail would be the staples of British life for generations to come. The state industries would become mammoth employers. The National Health Service alone would employ over a million workers in just a couple of decades. Assimilation under the state umbrella brought the burden of management. As the new state employees organized for improved pay and conditions, the trade union movement found fertile ground for recruiting and mobilizing a massive new membership. The national union of mineworkers, the transport and general workers' union, and the steelworkers' union would become synonymous with strikes, picket lines, and industrial unrest.

The workers in the new National Health Service would have a union of its very own: the Confederation of Health Service Employees, or COHSE, who would prove their mettle at the picket line.

A blizzard of legislation had been passed to slay Beveridge's five giants, some, such as education, with considerable success, but none without considerable cost to the state. One giant, however, would prove particularly difficult to slay. For the next generation, as successive financial crises hit Britain and unemployment rose to a staggering 3.5 million in the 1970s, the giant "Idleness" would continue to lumber through Britain at will.

Chapter 3

THE JEWEL IN THE WELFARE CROWN

"ON MONDAY MORNING WE WILL WAKE UP IN A NEW Britain, in a state which 'takes over' its citizens six months before they are born, providing care and free services for their birth, for their early years, their schooling, sickness, workless days, widowhood and retirement, all this with free doctoring, dentistry and medicine. You begin paying next Friday." Thus the *Daily Mail* heralded the arrival of the welfare state on the Appointed Day, Monday July 5, 1948.

The task of planning and implementing the National Health Service fell to Aneurin Bevan, the hot-tempered Welsh Labor MP for Ebbw Vale. Born in 1897, one of thirteen children of a Welsh miner, Bevan himself started working down the coal pit at the age of thirteen. Rising through the ranks of the local coal mining trade unions, he helped organize the Welsh miners in the general strike of 1926, at the age of twenty-nine. Three years later, he was elected as the Labor MP for Ebbw Vale. At thirty-three years of age, the youngest MP in the House of Commons, Bevan began one of the most controversial and colorful careers of any modern-day Labor politician. His oratory skills, in spite of a high squeaky voice with a thick Welsh lilt, were legendary. His hot temper and volatile temperament were folklore and, in 1939, would lead to his (temporary) banishment from his own Labor benches.

His tirades against Winston Churchill and the coalition government during the war would cause his Labor colleagues to wince at their venom, which bordered near treason. In 1951, he would retire in a bad-tempered protest against charges that were to be implemented for glasses and false teeth provided from "his" National Health Service. Nonetheless, he was a leading light in the Labor movement and was widely considered prime ministerial material, were it not for his stormy temperament and his spontaneous outbursts. In spite of his working class background and his ceaseless campaigning of the common man, he developed a taste for London society life. Aided and abetted by Lord Beaverbrook, newspaper baron and man-about-town, this unlikely duo did the party rounds of London's social elite. His newfound liking for the London "good life" was to earn him the nickname of the "Bollinger Bolshevik."

As a member of the Labor Party during the war years, he was a fierce critic of Churchill and his conduct of the war. In September of 1939, with the loss of Tobruk, and with Rommel and the Africa Corp fifty miles from El Alamein, Bevan proposed a motion of no confidence in Churchill's conduct of the war. The decisive battle of El Alamein was four weeks away. On the floor of the House of Commons, Bevan accused Churchill of incompetence and of "winning every debate in the house, yet losing every battle." His anti-Churchill diatribe was electrifying, and even Churchill, defending himself on the floor of the Commons, congratulated Bevan on his performance. The motion of no confidence in Churchill and the government was defeated by 475 votes to 25. The animosity was mutual. Churchill referred to him as "a squalid nuisance" and mentioned Bevan once in his six-volume epic on the Second World War. With the election of Attlee's Labor government in 1945, Bevan was appointed minister of health, a post that, at the time, also included responsibility for local government and housing. Clement Attlee understood the need to keep his Welsh firebrand occupied with as much responsibility and workload as could be placed on him. He was not to be disappointed.

Bevan's National Health Service did not develop in a vacuum. The Medical Planning Commission, the think tank of the British Medical Association (BMA), had proposed the concept of a nationalized health service, administered and funded by local government, in 1942, months before the Beveridge Report. The BMA polled the medical community, and of the twenty-seven thousand doctors who replied, a majority, 52 percent, were in favor of a postwar National Health Service. The same general principle for a local government-run health service had been proposed in a number of reports between 1943 and 1945 by the coalition government. There was already precedent for local government control of a national health service. County governments already ran the municipal hospitals, and they were responsible for the public health service, managed by the medical officers of health. In addition, local government administered a vast "institutional" service, responsible for long-term confinement of the elderly and disabled, and ran all the psychiatric hospitals.

The principle of a local government–run National Health Service has been proposed as far back as 1919 in a Labor Party planning document, which originally coined the term

National Health Service. One year later, in 1920, Lord Dawson, recently discharged from the military, reviewed organization of health care in Britain, and published the Dawson Report, which proposed a broadly similar plan for the reorganization of Britain's health service based on local government organization and administration.

By 1935, the municipal hospitals provided the vast majority of inpatient care, and the voluntary hospitals catered to a smaller and more affluent circle. The municipal hospitals accounted for 60 percent of health care expenditure in Britain, the voluntary hospitals consumed 20 percent, and the National Health Insurance Plan, providing the services of GPs and panel doctors, another 20 percent. Prior to Bevan, central government control of the health service had not been considered seriously, and it was widely thought that it might "interfere with the well-tested machinery of local government as it is already known." The new minister of health, Aneurin Bevan, also had responsibility for local government and realized its shortcomings at an early stage. Many local authorities were notoriously reactionary; others were simply incapable of taking on the task. The doctors were also against local government running of the hospitals, because of their very varied abilities and because the specter of the old Poor Law still hung above the municipal hospitals.

Bevan sought to spread the net wider and administer his new health service on a broader geographical basis, to dilute the influence of individual local governments. Health "regions" were created, incorporating several counties, the seat of local government. The regions were to be the self-contained administrative units of the new NHS. During World War II, when hospitals doctors and the ambulance service were taken over by the central government under the Emergency Medical Service, Britain had been divided into these same regions. England and Wales were divided into ten, London into four, each radiating from the city center, to facilitate evacuation. Bevan understood the control of the hospitals was central to his controlling the physicians and, ultimately, implementing his National Health Service.

In 1945, the hospitals, "the medical high ground," consisted of seventeen hundred municipal hospitals and thirteen hundred voluntary hospitals. By World War II, the municipal hospitals received 40 percent of their funding from central government. The voluntary hospitals relied on contributions solicited from wealthy donors and fundraising by local philanthropists. "Flag days" were frequent events, when nurses would take to the streets, rattling tin cans for donations in return for a lapel "flag" pin. Hospitals came in all shapes and sizes, containing from six to over a thousand beds. Together with the municipals and voluntary hospitals, small towns often boasted a "cottage" hospital with a few beds; others had built "memorial" hospitals for World War I veterans. Each was independent of its neighbor and frequently competed for donations to remain afloat. At the outset of World War II, the Ministry of Health compiled a list of hospitals some three thousand long and organized them on a regional basis under the Emergency Hospitals Scheme.

Surveyors from the Ministry of Health then set out to evaluate each of these institutes to determine what each was capable of handling. It was the first review ever of Britain's hospitals and would result in a comprehensive dossier known as the "Doomsday Report," providing an inventory of each hospital and a blueprint for future reorganizing of the health service. The last time any such survey had been conducted was the workhouse inspection by the assistant Poor Law commissioners. Starting with London, Andrew Topping, the MOH for London City Council, and Archibald Grey, a dermatologist, set out across England in the footsteps of the assistant Poor Law commissioners over a hundred years earlier, to review the hospital situation first hand. In all, fourteen survey teams (usually consisting of two doctors and a hospital administrator) set out, one to each region and assessed each of the three thousand establishments that considered themselves a hospital. The survey found a "hodgepodge" array of competing and conflicting hospitals with no rhyme or reason for their location or service. It was obvious that integration was required, and resources within each region should be centralized. "Petty rivalries should cease," warned Archibald Gray in anticipation of the outcry from the embattled hospitals. Smaller hospitals were integrated or closed, their nursing and auxiliary staffs transferred. Services such as radiology or pathology were added where necessary. It was a radical reorganization that would set the stage for Bevan's hospital plan over a decade later.

World War II had demonstrated that the voluntary hospital system was no longer viable. Many had been damaged or destroyed, and the war had dried up much of the fervor for voluntary donations of cash. The demise of the voluntary hospitals was not from poor management or poor care. They had a much better reputation for cleanliness, staff discipline, and overall quality of care than the municipals. Admission to a voluntary hospital required either money or a letter from a contributor, to make a case for his treatment. The voluntaries were able to pick and choose who was admitted to their wards, so chronic patients, with little chance of recovery or cure, were avoided, to keep beds available. Indigent patients would be admitted if their condition was rare or interesting since they provided valuable teaching cases. If they became a chronic, long-term problem, they were transferred to the local municipal hospital. The voluntary hospitals were stand-alone organizations, wholly dependent on voluntary contributions and bequeathments. The municipals could rely on a steadier income and were funded by the local rates and block grants from Westminster. Lacking government subsidy, a downturn in the nation's financial health would place the voluntary hospitals in a precarious situation, as it did in 1945.

Both the voluntary and the municipal hospital systems had been assimilated under the Emergency Medical Service during the war, and the system had worked well. The Emergency Medical System proved to be a dress rehearsal for the National Health Service. Bevan, who refused to discuss his plans with the medical community before he had an element of parliamentary approval, decided on central government organization and funding of the health service for two reasons. First was to throw wide the net to incorporate several local authorities, thereby diminishing the power of the individual authority. The appointment of community leaders to the regional hospital board, the governing body of the region, would also dilute the influence of the local physicians, who were hostile to Bevan and his steamroller tactics. Second was that funding of the health service by central government through general taxation would maximize funding from the Treasury, as opposed to relying on the local rate system.

Organization of the physicians proved more problematic. The senior hospital doctors, or consultants, realized they required a hospital system in which to practice their art. They were a more captive population than the general practitioners who practiced in the community, often from a room in their own homes. The consultants acquiesced to a full-time salaried service more readily than the GPs, so long as the purse strings were not held by the local government. The British Medical Association, whose membership consisted mostly of GPs, were opposed to a full-time salaried service for physicians and held a series of plebiscites, the first of which was slated for January 1948. The terms of Bevan's first plan for a National Health Service, released in 1946, called for a full-time salaried service for all physicians, including GPs. Private practice by hospital consultants was to be banned. The long-standing practice of retiring GPs to sell their practices to younger doctors, known then, as now, as the "goodwill" system, was banished. Bevan took his usual negotiating stance and refused to "alter one word" of his original proposal, confirming the physicians' fears that Bevan had not moved far from the pit head of the Welsh coal mines. Relationships between BMA in Tavistock House and the Ministry of Health in Richmond House chilled. The Appointed Day was just over six months away. As the autumn of 1947 turned into a bitter winter, the political climate also took a turn for the worse. Bevan accused the BMA leadership of being "politically poisoned and raucous voiced." The BMA, in turn, referred to their new minister of health as "like Hitler, utterly evil" and "a totalitarian dictator."

As the winter gales of 1947 raged outside, the bitter exchanges between Bevan and the BMA continued in a series of very public exchanges. The winter months, the worst that century, brought gales and blizzards on an unprecedented scale. The snow and frost killed thousands of farm animals, leading to an already critical food shortage. Coal and fuel oil were in short supply, adding to the frozen misery. The "big freeze" of 1948 led to a bitterly cold spring of 1948, with torrential rains, the wettest in a hundred years. Floods destroyed farms and villages and delayed planting of much-needed crops. Food rationing became even more stringent than anyone had seen during the war years. The meat ration was halved, and for the first time, staples such as bread and potatoes were rationed. It seemed the elements themselves were conspiring against the high-minded ambitions of His Majesty's Labor government.

During the negotiations, Bevan demonstrated characteristic intransigence and refused to change a word of the original act. With the deadline of July 5, 1948, rapidly approaching, the press, who sided with Bevan and an eager public, covered the standoff. The BMA organized a plebiscite, the first of two which would eventually be held, to determine the will of its membership. The first plebiscite was scheduled for January 1948. The results were a landslide victory for the BMA. In a nine-to-one majority, with 84 percent of physicians responding, the medical profession rejected Mr. Bevan's terms for the new health service. With the realization that his new health service would be without doctors, Bevan's attitude changed overnight. Compromises were struck. Consultants would be allowed to participate in private practice but on a very restricted basis. The consultants' week was divided into eleven half days (including Saturday morning). Each consultant could decide either to work full time for the NHS or part time. Those not wishing to pursue private practice and who elected to work full time for the NHS signed an "eleven-elevenths" contract, for which they would receive a full-time salary. Those wishing to continue private practice on the side became "maximum part-time" employees, spending nine-elevenths of their time with the

NHS, thus leaving two half days for their private practice. The NHS "maximum part-time" salaries were cut proportionately. Furthermore, private patients could be admitted to the National Health Service hospitals and be charged for their stay. As an incentive to the full-time consultants, a system of merit awards was introduced: These were cash bonuses designed to reward particularly outstanding physicians or in recognition of long years of service. Various grades of merit awards were established, the highest (and rarest) could double a consultant's salary; however, few physicians received them, and the selection process was shrouded in secrecy. Although it was intended that this compensate for foregoing private practice, it was not a reality for the vast majority of doctors. Ironically, the secrecy surrounding the awards process generated resentment for many hardworking physicians in some of the less prestigious hospitals isolated from the awards process.

The general practitioners extracted even greater concessions from Mr. Bevan. Rejected were the full-time salaried service and the status of employee to the state. The general practitioners would attain the status of individual contractors to the National Health Service, reimbursed on a capitation basis, based on the old National Insurance Plan, and with bonuses for extra responsibilities such as immunizations and inner-city practices. Local health departments run by the medical officers of health remained largely unchanged. Administered by local government, they would continue in their current roles of monitoring infectious disease and food and water safety. Three separate and distinct tiers, therefore, evolved: the hospitals and their consultant specialists, the general practitioners in the community, and the local health departments.

This three-tier system was not ideal and effectively tripled administration and bureaucracy. Instead of fourteen integrated and self-sufficient regions covering the entire spectrum of health care, the new National Health Service would have some seven hundred separate administrative elements, with little or no crossover between them. The general practitioners, although retaining their independence, would be regarded as "potential delinquents" by Mr. Bevan and his administration. Retribution was swift. As an incentive to join his health service (on his terms), Bevan had proposed building two hundred health centers in cities throughout Britain, where delivery of health care by large groups of GPs would be made more efficient. After the second round of negotiations, these plans were scotched. Realistically, the critical shortage of building materials and the priority for rebuilding homes had made this a somewhat hollow promise from the outset. As a result of the new deal, the general practitioners, having retained their independence, were effectively barred from hospital practice and would continue their "immeasurable art" from rooms and offices dotted throughout the community.

With these concessions in hand, a second plebiscite was held in April of 1948, less than three months before launch day. In the second plebiscite, two out of three doctors disapproved of the amending act, with a total of 77 percent of physicians responding. However, the second question in the plebiscite asked this: "Would you serve in the new National Health Service?" To this, 12,799 indicated that they would, and 13,891 said they would not. The BMA had sought an absolute majority of no votes before it would reject Mr. Bevan's proposals a second (and probably final) time. With only a 77 percent turnout for the second vote, the 52 percent nos did not include a large block of general practitioners, who were the primary contestants in this battle. The result was, therefore, equivocal at best. The absolute majority that the BMA required had not been realized. The medical profession had acquiesced to the amended plan by default. In spite of his victory, Bevan had earned the distrust of the physicians, which would be not easily forgotten. After Bevan resigned as minister of health in 1951, an editorial in the *British Medical Journal* bid him farewell with the words, "His vicious attacks upon the profession, his attempts to sow discord, and his intransigence in negotiation would never be forgotten. He never rose above being a clever politician and at critical moments failed to become the statesmen. He has done his best to make himself disliked by the medical profession and, by and large, he succeeded."

Under the new regional plan, Britain was divided into ten regional health authorities, each one associated with a major university. London was divided into four regions, for a total of fourteen throughout Britain and Wales. Each region was divided into a health district, seventy-five in all, and each district divided into area health authorities, 120 in England and Wales. Financing for the hospitals was based on expenditures during the course of the last two years and in the first six months of 1948. Financing, which had been provided by the local rates for the municipal hospitals, and from charitable contributions for the voluntary hospitals, was now provided by the Treasury. The more affluent hospitals in the south of England, therefore, maintained their edge over the provincial hospitals in the north, and this differential would persist for decades to come. The hospital consultants became salaried employees but were free to care for private patients two half days a week. Rather than lose potential revenue by refusing admission of private patients to NHS beds, Bevan acquiesced by earmarking a small number of "private beds" in NHS hospitals, which, in turn, derived revenue from the practice.

One concession that general practitioners were unable to extract from Bevan was the right to buy and sell their medical practices. In the years preceding the National Health Service, retiring physicians had been able to sell their practices to newly qualified doctors, known as the "goodwill" of the practice, typically amounting to one and a half times the retiring physician's annual salary. The newly qualified physician would take out a bank loan or pay off the loan in installments. In the new health service, this practice was banned. New physicians, rather than buying into the practice, found themselves as supplicants, often spending a considerable number of years (usually twelve years) before achieving parity as a senior partner. GPs in established practice on the Appointed Day were now reimbursement on a capitation basis. Since the entire population was required to sign up with a GP within a few weeks, newly qualified doctors found it impossible to set up a new practice, there being few if any "unassigned" patients left. Every new opening for a junior post in general practice received a hundred eager applicants. The number of general practitioners in England had been effectively capped. Ironically, GPs in poor inner city areas suddenly found their incomes boosted by virtue of the large population they served. GPs in small but affluent communities, accustomed to the old fee-for-service scheme, faced a sharp drop in income, based on the relatively small head count of their patients.

The concept of the new health service was an unqualified success with the general population. Within four weeks of its launch, 97 percent of the population had signed up with a GP. Doctors' surgeries were inundated with patients who, for the first time, had free access to a physician, together with free spectacles, false teeth, wigs, and a seeming panacea of benefits. Several months after the launch of the scheme, a frustrated general practitioner wrote to the *British Medical Journal*, "Evidence comes in from all over the country that doctors' surgeries are crowded out, the doctors themselves deplore that this heavy pressure of work has made it at times impossible for them to give the patients adequate care and attention. In the event of an epidemic in the winter, the life of the general practitioner, in particular, will become intolerable." Another GP wrote shortly after, "The situation is still too confused to get anything like a clear picture of what is happening, though perhaps the most noteworthy fact is the eagerness with which the public has sought to take advantage of a service which in effect guarantees the supply, free of charge, of everything from wigs to iron lungs."

A health service, accessible to all, irrespective of means, providing comprehensive benefits, and free at the point of consumption, has been an article of faith for the British people for the past fifty years. Nonetheless, two major characteristics of the health service—first, its party political stripes, and second, its funding from direct taxation—have left the National Health Service mired in the political arena. Being a favorite topic of party political rancor, meaningful changes in the National Health Service have been few. Even the smallest intrusions into the NHS are subject to contentious debate. Changes are usually a result of the political process, rather than a reflection of changing health care needs. Bevan was careful to earmark the National Health Service a creation of the Labor Party, and even fifty years later, the Labor Party portrays itself as the only trustworthy guardians of its safekeeping, in spite of their being in office for a minority of its years.

Funding of the health service from direct taxation can be seen as a double-edged sword. Any significant increase in services would mean a massive increase in the taxation rate and inevitable political consequences for its authors. Conversely, funding of the health service from direct taxation has limited budget increases to 2 or 3 percentage points per annum, figures that many Western nations, especially the United States, would find hard to comprehend. Beyond health care, Bevan also affected a redistribution of wealth on a much greater scale than had funding been provided through the existing National Insurance Plan or another contribution scheme.

The year 1948 certainly brought a redistribution of wealth for Britain, not between themselves, but among the major currencies of the world. The sterling crisis of 1948 resulted in a sharp devaluation of the pound, precipitated by the nation's economic quagmire. Since 1800, the dollar/pound rate had remained flat at five US dollars per pound. Even during national crises and war, such as the War of 1812, the pound slipped to $3.8, to rise again to $4. Even in 1945, the same rate of exchange prevailed. In 1948, burdened by war debt, with the devastation of much of its industrial infrastructure, the pound came under immense pressure and was devalued to a record low of $2.5. Financial assistance in the form of the Marshall Plan stabilized the currency, but the pound would never recover to former levels. Ironically, had it not been for the injection of US capital, the welfare state may never have been launched. Thirty years later, in 1976, the pound would find itself under pressure yet again, burdened by high unemployment and massive public expenditure, to maintain the nationalized industries and the welfare state. On this occasion, the exchange rate fell to $1.7, and intervention of the

International Monetary Fund was necessary to prevent further erosion. History would repeat itself once more in 1985, with the pound dropping to $1.15, again requiring intervention by the IMF. The burdens placed on the economy by massive public expenditure, low productivity in the nationalized industries, and rampant industrial unrest brought about a sea change in public opinion. The charge was led by the daughter of self-dependence and industrial privatization, Margaret Thatcher.

On the morning of July 5, 1948, however, Britain had moved closer to the bosom of the state. Britons were now eligible for free health care, guaranteed unemployment disability and sickness benefits, child benefits, maternity benefits, widow's benefits, and even funeral benefits: "cradle-to-grave" benefits in every meaning of the phrase. Britain's headlong plunge into the welfare state would last but one term of Clement Atlee's Labor government, to be replaced four years later by a conservative victory under the now aging Winston Churchill.

Ironically, the first political victim claimed by the National Health Service would be its founder himself, Aneurin Bevan. In 1951, faced with escalating health crisis, charges were imposed on patients receiving spectacles and false teeth from the National Health Service. Bevan resigned as minister of health in a bad-tempered tirade launched against his own Labor government, which he felt were mismanaging "his health service." According to a fellow cabinet member, Tony Benn, who was present for the performance, he "shook with rage and screamed. … The megalomania and neurosis and hatred and jealousy he displayed astounded us all." The National Health Service had claimed its first political victim. There would be many more to follow.

Chapter 4

THE WAITING LIST

HAVING DECIDED TO ENTER INTO A SURGICAL CAREER, I decided I needed to be at the center of things. I had one of two locations I needed to be in: the first, London, the location of the Royal College of Surgeons of England, and the second, Edinburgh, home of the Royal College of Surgeons of Edinburgh. I applied for surgical jobs at both locations and set out for my first job offer in Edinburgh, some six hours' drive north.

I set out from the farm in my aging Ford Escort, heading north along the A64 through the two-lane country roads of the north of England and the Border regions, into Scotland. Passing through Corbridge, the Roman fortress on Hadrian's Wall, the ancient border between Roman England and Pictish Scotland; through Jedburgh, past its ancient, crumbling ruins of Jedburgh Cathedral; past Alnwick Castle, seat of the Earl of Northumberland and movie location for many Harry Potter movies; across the River Tweed, the modern-day border between Scotland and England; and finally past the harbor town of Dunbar and then Haddington into the fertile plains of southern Scotland. My first interview was in the Royal Infirmary of Edinburgh (RIE), the flagship hospital of Scotland, and blocks away from the Royal College of Surgeons. I stopped off at a country pub in the Border region to eat lunch and have a local beer. Although amusing in retrospect, the beer was so good that I decided I was going to work in Edinburgh and never even traveled to London to interview.

On my first day as a surgical registrar in Edinburgh, I drove up to the imposing façade of the Royal Infirmary of Edinburgh. Built in 1736, the architecture was built on a grand scale and was stunning. Its Gothic frame was studded by pinnacled towers, reminiscent of a French chateau. The French and Scots were longtime allies against the English, and their architecture often shared that history. A massive central clock tower was the central focus for the impressive building, which was built on a herringbone plan with a central corridor, the spine of the building, and each of its twelve wards jutting out as limbs at right angles on each side of the building.

The forecourt was guarded by a massive double wrought-iron gate that was rolled open and closed by the formal black-uniformed, gold-buttoned hospital doorman, Jimmy, whom I grew to know very well. From the forecourt, I climbed the massive stone stairs to the oak double doors that opened into a massive marble-floored lobby dwarfed by a spiral oak staircase that wound up to the first level of the hospital. The marble floor featured the image of a huge pelican, with its beak tucked under its wing, the emblem of the RIE nursing school, the graduates of which are still known as "The Pelicans." The significance was, so I was told, that in facing starvation, the mother pelican plucks tissue from its own breast in order to feed its young.

An ornate, three-hundred-year-old oak panel listed the names of the benefactors who had donated generously to the foundation of the hospital. I ascended the stairs to find my future home for the next several years, Wards Five and Six of the Royal Infirmary, the general surgery unit. The wards were based on the eighteenth-century Florence Nightingale pattern, with twelve beds lining each side of the long wall, making each bed clearly visible at all times. On entering the ward, the surgeons' offices were located off to the side, the staff room, the kitchen, and the sisters' office, who ran the nursing staff under the direction of the matron. The Royal Infirmary was built on a massive scale. There had been few remodeling attempts since it was last updated in 1830, other than an ancient hot water boiler system that cranked day and night, feeding heat into the wrought iron radiators stationed between each of the patient's beds and beneath huge, arched windows that allowed the dwindling sunlight of the northern city to filter into the wards.

The operating theater (operating room) was built on a similar eighteenth-century scale and had seen even fewer renovations. The central oval marble floor was surrounded on half its circumference by oak trestle seats (bleachers) for the ancient eighteenth- and nineteenth-century surgeons to eagerly watch the earliest operations, leaning over the oak handrail in their black frock coats and dripping beards to stare at the procedure beneath them. Leading into the theater, there were two anterooms where patients were wheeled into the operating theater for surgery and then wheeled out into the second, a recovery room, after the performance. In the corner of the theater, a marble sink stood, with a single (cold) water faucet, which served as a scrub sink. A stainless steel bowl, filled with alcohol, served as the final step for scrubbing prior to surgery. As I was to find out, the alcohol bowl also served as a stinging reminder to remind me of any cut or scrape I had on my hands, when the cuts were exposed to absolute alcohol. I had seen these operation rooms previously, but only in eighteenth-century oil portraits of Theodor Billroth, the grandfather of surgery; David Hunter, the nineteenth-century surgical pioneer; and Alexander Fleming, the father of antisepsis.

On day one, having introduced myself to my new colleagues, acclimatizing myself to the new surroundings and settling into a new and demanding environment, I started to settle down into the routine that would be my life for the next two years. The senior surgeon, Ian B. McLeod, (IBM) was a wiry, dour Scot, and was, without a doubt, the best surgeon I have ever met. He was a man of few words, he chain-smoked unfiltered Capstan full-strength cigarettes between cases, and he had a dry, if not arid, sense of humor. He talked little, smiled less, and never laughed, earning his nickname, "Zip Lip." He was not a man to be trifled with. His erstwhile secretary, Sheileigh, an all-knowing, all-seeing, all-doing multitasker, had been his secretary for decades. She was IBM's softer, gentler executive. Jolly, helpful, and bouncy, Sheileigh smoked the filtered version of IBM's favorite cigarette.

Having settled into the routine, and getting some degree of autonomy, I was permitted to have my own operating list for half a day. Anxious to get started and gain experience, I was eager to call patients to schedule them for their planned surgeries. Sheileigh directed me to the waiting list where my future patients could be found. Their contact numbers were available, and she would arrange all the details. She directed me to a small room adjoining her office where the "waiting list" resided. I was led into an oak-paneled, ten-by-twelve-foot room lined by oak filing drawers, obviously original to the 1860 renovations. "Here they are," she said and smiled, brandishing a wave toward the files. "Help yourself." she quipped. Each drawer contained dozens of index cards, each identifying a patient requiring surgery, filed by type of surgery needed and in order of waiting time on the list. This was no list. This was a library.

I slid open the appropriate drawers and excitedly started to select my first list of patients to offer them surgery. Just little procedures first: hernias, gallbladders, varicose veins. I started to select patients who had been on the waiting list the longest and picked up the phone to schedule them to come in for their surgery. Many people had been on the waiting list for years, and I was expecting an unequivocal "Yes! I'll be there." I was shocked when, all too routinely, an elderly female with a lilting Scot's voice answered the phone, and, after being asked if Mr. McDonald, Mr. McDougal, Mr. Sinclair, or whatever their name would like to have his surgery performed the following week, all too often the reply was "Oh, I'm sorry, my dear. He died years ago." I duly apologized, exchanged the usual pleasantries, and went to the next index card. This happened so many times I decided to start from the front of the list, since there was, at least, a better chance that these people would still be alive.

Part of my surgical responsibilities was to cover the emergency room every fourth weekday night and every fourth weekend. The emergency room covered a major-sized urban community in the southeast of Scotland and was one of the busiest in the country. Like most emergency rooms, it was busy day and night. Friday and Saturday nights were prime time for drunken brawls, car accidents, and the resulting injuries. Winters were always busier with hip fractures and wrist fractures from the citizens of Edinburgh slipping on the ever-present ice on pavements (sidewalks). Car wrecks from the Border Region, fifty miles south, came in frequently. The emergency room served the entire population, from the humblest street persona to the elders of the city. I realized at an early stage that the promise of the NHS, "from cradle to grave, from duke to dustman," was a reality.

For acute emergencies, the protocol for a patient walking into the emergency room and providing a name and address, gaining access to see a doctor, being treated for their injury or ailment, and leaving treated or with plans to do so, went something like this: there was none. The protocol was, and is, a strict first-come, first-served system. There was, and is, no insurance information required, no social security number needed, no employer information requested, no guarantor information, and basically, no nothing. As promised, the National Health Service was, and is, free for all at the point of service. There is no means-testing; medical records were basic and rudimentary, but treatment was as up to date as any other hospital in England or Scotland, or for that matter, in any other European nation. The emergency room was broadly divided into a medical area and a surgical area. The Accident and Emergency (A&E) duty "sister" (charge nurse) triaged patients to the medical or surgical area depending on their complaints, based typically on her often decades of experience. Ambulance patients, unconscious victims of regular brawls, serious fractures, or bad car wrecks were shunted immediately to the trauma room. For routine patients, the emergency room was lined by wooden chairs where the most unkempt street person would routinely be seen slumped next to a mink-clad socialite.

One busy Saturday night, being assigned to the surgical area, I was treating a young adolescent male who had sustained a wrist fracture. His concerned mother, well-dressed, well-groomed, and clearly well-educated, was in attendance at all times. The kid needed a plaster splint on his wrist, and I dutifully took him to the plaster area, ready to apply the splint under anesthesia. I glanced momentarily at his chart, about to address his mother and explain what I was about to do. The name was very familiar, the same as one of Margaret Thatcher's government ministers then currently in power. I gave the mom a puzzled look, furrowed my brow, and asked the simple question, "Any relation?" She smiled and nodded and said simply, "Dad." Even the families of sitting government ministers checked in the same way as the humblest homeless citizens of the city and, at least in this case, neither expected nor received priority treatment.

There was no lack of cases from the emergency room. Minor traumas, lacerations, fractures, and head injuries were interspersed with major and immediate surgical emergencies such as perforated ulcers, perforated colons, and GI bleeding from duodenal ulcers, a side effect of the heavy smoking and heavy drinking population. The OR ran all day and all night, and the surgical "registrar of the day" performed all the surgeries. Lacking any extensive surgical experience, I spent my time operating on these individuals divided between absolute sheer fascination and sheer horror, as I operated on patients in the operating theater all hours of the day and night, with a surgical textbook open at the relevant page, within a foot or two of the action. To call for help from a senior surgeon was a sign of weakness and probably a career ender unless it was a life-and-death situation. Guns (firearms) were illegal in Britain at that time, and I didn't see a single gunshot wound in the years I spent there. Though plenty of stabbings, head injuries from bludgeoning, the occasional enucleated eye from a spurned girlfriend, and even an ax fight, which spilled into the emergency room from outside Lauriston Place, I saw not a single gunshot wound.

New Year's Eve in Edinburgh (Hogmanay) was particularly memorable. I came on duty at nine o'clock in the evening, expecting the place to be packed. The place was empty, not a soul to be seen. The stretchers (gurneys) had been removed from the emergency room, to be replaced by mattresses laid on the ground in neat rows. Buckets of sawdust were positioned between each of the mattresses. I was told how the New Year's Eve protocol would work. The emergency room would be quiet until a few minutes after midnight when the celebrating Scots lasted until the stroke of midnight, when they passed out either drunk, severely injured, with a head injury, or a combination of all three. The protocol was as follows: Unconsciousness individuals were laid on the mattresses, checked for neck injuries, external injuries, and examined quickly head to toe, rolled over to check for knife wounds, before moving to the next victim. As the patient sobered up, they usually rolled over, typically vomited between the mattresses, whereupon the sawdust was thrown over the vomit to be cleaned up later. I was a little shocked, but this seemed like an efficient system. Sure enough, a few minutes after midnight the familiar two-tone whine of the ambulances could be heard approaching the hospital from the city center, with the first crop of New Year's revelers.

Aside from emergency surgeries, routine or elective cases were performed twice a week in the operating theater, between the hours of 9:00 a.m. and 3:00 p.m. The major cases came first: the cancers, the life-threatening conditions such as aneurysms and limb salvage. The senior consultant, IBM, would operate smoothly, effectively, silently, and with superb skill throughout the day, punctuated only an unfiltered Capstan full-strength cigarette between cases. As the clock approached three in the afternoon, the anesthesiologist would become restless, look over to see how the case was progressing, and announce that three o'clock was rapidly approaching. However ambitious, however anxious any surgeon was to work through the afternoon into the evening, the anesthesiologists, nurses, and ancillary staff were paid for eight hours, and eight hours it would be. Any cases left over were wheeled back to the floor where they returned to their beds to wait for the next operating list in two or three days' time. This common and highly inefficient means of making sure the OR list remained intact was referred to as "bed blocking." If a surgical patient was not in the bed, inevitably a patient with pneumonia or other chronic medical condition would take up the precious bed, and gradually the case list for the next operating day dwindled or disappeared.

Surgical rounds in Wards Five and Six of the Royal Infirmary were led by IBM, twice a week, after finishing the operating list. Being a man of few words, he had little or no time to have in-depth discussions with concerned family members. Entering Wards Five and Six with his entourage, IBM would summon the ward sister, who would stride down the length of the ward, clap her hands, and ask all family members to leave the floor until after rounds were completed. IBM, myself, and the rest of the team would then go from bed to bed, issue orders, and move seamlessly up and down the floors. Although clearly lacking any family sensitivity, this was a supremely efficient way of treating patients.

Many of the patients on the ward had complex pathologies as a result of little or no preexisting medical care and the usual laissez-faire Scots attitude. Many of these patients required CT scans to help diagnose the problem prior to operating on them. Attempting to obtain a CT scan for a complex ward patient was one of the most frustrating processes in a system that was peppered with frustrations and inefficiencies.

Ironically, the CT scan was a British invention from start to finish. The CT scan was developed in the 1970s by Dr. Hounsfield, a Brit. Funds for the research came from EMI, another British company, the record label for the Beatles. EMI was flush with cash after a string of record-breaking hits by the Beatles, and they diversified their portfolio from making music into research involving medical imaging, including the CT scan. In its early days, CT scans were few and far between, and requests for CT scan were vetted thoroughly before approval. If patients required the scan, it would routinely be at least two days to a week until a scan could be completed. This is yet another block caused by inefficiencies in the system. It struck me as ironic that the CT scan, developed in Britain, by a Brit, funded by a British company, would be so out of reach for the National Health Service.

The 1970s were also blighted by industrial unrest in Britain. A series of inept Labor governments and radical unions, under the umbrella of the Trades Union Council, (TUC) embarked on a bitter and prolonged fight against the British government for higher wages and improved working conditions. The

1970s were peppered by several winters of discontent marred by transport strikes, coal miner strikes, power worker strikes, hospital ancillary strikes, ambulance strikes, laundry strikes, and nursing strikes. An already inefficient system was bogged down by an environment of political unrest, work-to-rules, go-slows, and picketing.

When the laundry workers went on strike, there was no laundry, and therefore OR lists were canceled. When the coal miners, transport workers, or power workers went on strike, electricity supplies were curtailed. No surgeries. When the ancillary staff went on strike, there was no cleaning or maintenance of the hospital. No surgeries. When the ambulance men went on strike, the patients, who were brought to outpatient clinics in ambulances, for reasons I could never comprehend, could not attend clinics, further adding to the waiting lists. When nurses went on strike, the whole place shut down.

Against this backdrop of frustration, inefficiencies, and uncertainty was the process of fulfilling a career as a surgeon and reaching elusive and much-coveted senior post as a consultant. The hierarchy of surgical ranks went from the lowly houseman to senior house officer to registrar to senior registrar, finally reaching the pinnacle of a consultant position. The number of consultant posts in Britain was finite and fixed. Meanwhile, the ranks of the underlings kept the NHS system ticking over. Many left the ranks before reaching consultant and instead entered radiology or general practice, or threw in the towel and emigrated to Australia, New Zealand, or Canada.

Such was the organization system of the National Health Service that it was necessary to find a new position every year or so, through the appointment section of the *British Medical*

Journal. This led to a very uncertain, very insecure career for an aspiring surgeon. Funds from the National Health Service were fixed, and therefore there were no new consultant spots. Basically, the backlog of junior surgeons literally waited for consultants to retire or die. Once reaching the consultant level, the National Health Service allowed consultants one and a half days of the week to perform what private practice they wished to do so. It was unlawful for any junior member to entire private practice. A young surgeon's career was very uncertain and very volatile. The only certainty was there would be plenty of patients on the waiting list, if only we could actually operate on them.

Chapter 5

THE THREE-LAYERED CAKE: THE GENESIS OF US STATE MEDICINE

ON THREE SEPARATE OCCASIONS DURING THE LAST hundred years, the stage has been set in US politics for the introduction of comprehensive, nationalized health care. On each of these occasions, the pendulums of the judiciary, the legislative, and executive branches come into alignment to make such a radical plan a reality. However, only on one occasion, during the Johnson Administration, with a liberal Democratic-dominated Congress and a sympathetic judiciary, did any such plan come to fruition. Even during the radical liberal reforms of the Johnson, the enacted health reforms fell far short of comprehensive nationalized health care. The second occasion where nationalized health care appeared is beyond the brink of reality, during the Republican administration of Richard Nixon. The events of history intervened in the form of Watergate, which scuttled Nixon's initiatives, and smothered hopes of a nationalized health plan for at least two decades. (One cynical view points to the Nixon health reform proposals as a decoy action to divert attention away from the ultimately fatal Watergate scandal besetting his administration.) The third opportunity came in the early years of the Clinton administration, whose basic proposals were not far removed from those of Nixon. The ambitions for an employer-funded, mandatory health care system used the private sector (HMOs and indemnity insurance plans) as the engines of his reform, administered by a federal health czar. An inexperienced president, already weakened by his attempt to implement a campaign promise to introduce gays into the military, Clinton was to make a strategic error in appointing his wife as federal health care czarina. Having banned the medical profession from any part of the process and isolating herself and the administration politically, the final blow was delivered when Clinton's own choice for America's doctor, the surgeon general, resigned after allegations of her own son's use of illegal drugs.

On three other occasions during the last century, public opinion swung heavily toward the need for nationalized medicine, but sustained political opposition, or the events of history, intervened to prevent its passage. During the final years of Franklin D. Roosevelt's unprecedented fourth term in office, and during the last months of his life, the father of American Social Security acquiesced to a national health care plan. Death intervened before his ambitions could be translated into reality. The dwindling hopes for American "socialized medicine" were resuscitated by Harry Truman but were ultimately defeated by a combination of unprecedented postwar prosperity and the lobbying efforts of the American Medical Association.

John F. Kennedy's New Frontier agenda made nationalized health care a "must-do" priority for his administration, although his plans died with him in Dallas, Texas. The ambitions of the martyred president would lay the groundwork for Johnson's unprecedented success in passing the current form of America's socialized medicine in the form of Medicare and Medicaid in 1965. The Carter administration, twenty years later, attempted to extend plans for a comprehensive nationalized health care in 1978, using the resurrected Nixon plan of four years earlier as its basis. However, the following year, Jimmy Carter's ambitions of enacting comprehensive health care were abducted with the American hostages in Tehran, an event which would bog down and ultimately sink his administration three years later.

In America, the call for state-provided health care came only as an extension to state-sponsored Social Security. In the arena of state-sponsored Social Security, the United States lagged twenty-five years behind Britain and almost fifty years behind state social security programs in Germany. In 1885, Chancellor Bismarck pushed through the first government-sponsored insurance plan against disability and unemployment for German workers, followed by a similar plan by Lloyd George in Britain in 1911. It was not until 1937 that the US Supreme Court changed its position from considering such plans as government interference in working conditions.

Since the beginning of the century, the conservative-minded Supreme Court struck down any considerations of federally sponsored unemployment or disability insurance as unwarranted government intrusion into employer-employee relationships. Their interpretations of the Ninth and Fourteenth Amendments held sway until the onset of the Great Depression and Roosevelt's introduction of the Social Security Act in 1937. If the conservative Supreme Court of the early decades of the nineteenth century considered the boots and gloves of working Americans as off-limits, then certainly their minds and bodies were strictly private affairs. Compared to the governments in England and Germany, the federal government in America at the turn of the century was geographically distant and politically at arm's length from the states. The federal government concentrated its attention on defense, foreign policy, and macroeconomics. Social welfare and health care were left to state and local governments, which in turn handed the responsibility to voluntary organizations and the church. By the turn of the century, federal aid for health care had been denied several times. In 1854, a national mental health bill was vetoed by President Pierce on the grounds of government intrusion into the individual's private affairs. In 1883, the National Board of Health was abolished after only four years in existence.

Entrepreneurs in the private sector experimented with underwriting policies for sickness benefits. One of the first of these fledgling insurance companies, the Prudential Insurance Company, founded in 1875 by John F. Dryden, met with little success. By the very complex nature of "sickness," Dryden found that evaluating and monitoring claimants proved too complex and time-consuming. He, therefore, returned to the more straightforward and predictable business of insurance coverage for funerals. The call for nationalized health insurance gained momentum in 1910 when the concept was championed by the Progressive Party. Choosing Teddy Roosevelt in his reelection bid as the presidential candidate, the Progressives campaign for state-run health and disability insurance was modeled after the German model. The defeat of Teddy Roosevelt to Woodrow Wilson set back the plans for nationalized health and social insurance. America's entry into World War I in 1917 effectively scuttled discussion of any "German" plan as outright treason.

The coming of the Great Depression, the election of the reformed-minded Franklin Roosevelt, and a more sympathetic Supreme Court set the stage for a federal social security plan. A committee on economic security was established in 1934. With the massive and increasing unemployment since 1929, its primary goal was to explore federal unemployment benefits. A secondary measure was to look into the feasibility of pensions. Health insurance, not the immediate national threat that unemployment represented, was relegated down the list. Even the possibility of a modest health insurance plan produced a sudden uproar from the American Medical Association and its members. Physicians were anxious to preserve their free enterprise system on a fee-for-service basis. Any subordination of this to an insurance middleman was seen as a loss of professional autonomy, not to mention a loss of financial control. Such was the furor from the medical profession that Roosevelt recognized that holding out for a federal health insurance plan would jeopardize passage of his entire Social Security bill. The act was, therefore, passed without any provision for federal health care whatsoever.

As the Great Depression dug deeper, however, many of the newly created federal agencies began introducing health care insurance in an indirect manner. The Farm Security Agency, for instance, negotiated reduced rates from the local physicians in rural areas to provide health care for the local farmers in the event they became ill. The motivation for the federal agencies was to avoid any lost farm income and resulting defaults on federal loans. For many physicians, a reduced fee was better than no fee at all. Consequently, the principle of federally funded health care entered via the back door of America's farmsteads.

Even though the provision for universal health care had been omitted from the Social Security Act of 1935, the concept did not die. Three years later, in 1938, Roosevelt appointed an interdepartmental committee to coordinate health and welfare activities, twelve months before Beveridge was appointed to an almost identical interdepartmental committee in Westminster, three thousand miles away. The committee called a conference to discuss the concept of nationalized health care to be held in Washington, DC, in July of 1938. The National Health Conference, the first of its kind to be held, made five recommendations that they considered cornerstones for the further development of an American health care system. These included a nationwide health care plan paid for by general taxation, a federally sponsored disability insurance program, federal grants for hospital building program, federal grants for maternal and child health care provision, and federal grants to state health care systems for indigents.

The principles were certainly not a clear plan of action, nor was there any general agreement on a federal- or state-run system; hence, the possibility of both was included in the five-point plan. Nonetheless, the AMA, for the second time in four years, convened an emergency meeting to discuss tactics. Again, the main objective was to avoid a compulsory insurance program which they had successfully defeated four years earlier in the Social Security plan. Meetings were held between the AMA and the interdepartmental committee, but little headway was made. Fortunately for the AMA, the midterm elections of 1938 brought an influx of Republican lawmakers into Congress. In addition, the Southern Democrats, the "Dixiecrats," balked at the concept of providing federal or state health care for all citizens equally since this would include the black population that was still laboring under conditions preceding the civil rights legislation. Roosevelt, therefore, found himself confronted not only by a dissenting Republican Party but also by a large contingent of his own Democratic Party.

Nonetheless, the concept of national health care was kept alive by the Northern Democrats, primarily Senator Wagner from New York, Representative Murray from Montana, and Representative Dingell from Michigan. Senator Robert Wagner was the son of an immigrant, who grew up in New York's downtrodden eastside. Wagner had strong labor ties and had a long history of investigating and proposing pro-labor legislation. Thirty years earlier, in 1911, he was involved in hearings into the Triangle Shirtwaist Company fire in New York City, where scores of workers had been burned to death. Ten years earlier, he was a member of a Senate subcommittee investigating the atrocious working conditions in America's coal mines. Senator Wagner was the sponsor of the 1936 Social Security Act and had played a major role in creating many of the New Deal programs during the Depression.

Wagner incorporated the five-point plan at the National Health Conference into an omnibus health bill that he introduced in February of 1939. The plan was to amend the Social Security Act to provide federal funds to incorporate the principles into a comprehensive health care system. The most important provision called for federal aid to the states, which would be encouraged to develop health insurance plans for their poor and indigent. The states would, therefore, have the primary responsibility of developing and running Wagner's health care plan. However, the year was 1939, and events on the global stage diverted the public's attention away from health care. Roosevelt, fresh from his run-in with organized medicine's opposition to his Social Security Act, was not keen to repeat the performance. In addition, the now conservative-dominated Congress was increasing its opposition to the New Deal programs, and any new massive federal health care plan would likely fail. The health reformists were, therefore, denied a second chance to implement their plans. As Hitler's Nazis marched into Poland in September of 1939, the plans for America's socialized medicine again gathered dust.

Although federally sponsored health care had died, the battle for health care continued at the state level. Legislation was introduced in thirteen states during the war years, and in Rhode Island, the health insurance movement scored its first victory. The Rhode Island legislature sponsored an insurance plan for state employees, which paid cash benefits during unemployment due to ill health. Similar measures were introduced at the level of local or city government. The largest of these was passed by New York City's reform-minded mayor, Fiorello La Guardia, in 1943. This radical plan, the Health Insurance Plan of Greater New York, provided health insurance to city workers and their dependents. The plan has survived the test of time and is one of the original, most successful government-sponsored plans to emerge in the United States.

The publication of the Beveridge Report in Britain in November of 1942 did not pass unnoticed in the United States, where thousands of copies were circulated. Parliament debated the Beveridge plan in February of 1943, and pro–National Health

Service statements by Churchill in a radio broadcast to Britain were also heard by attentive ears in the United States.

Senator Wagner saw his opportunity to reintroduce his health care legislation, this time assisted by Democratic Senator Murray and Representative Dingell. Senator James Murray had a personal interest in America's health care system since he had witnessed firsthand the impact of large-scale and chronic ill health in the form of pulmonary silicosis contracted by miners working in Montana's copper mines. Wagner, Murray, and Dingell revived the national health care debate by introducing the first of what would be a series of Wagner, Murray, and Dingell bills. The 1943 plan included provisions for unemployment insurance, old-age pensions, disability insurance, and most important, a comprehensive, nationalized, federally funded health care program. Although Wagner's 1939 bill had proposed a state-operated health care system, the 1943 version proposed a federal program.

Experience during the war had demonstrated the effectiveness of centralized planning and coordination. "We could not win the war with forty-eight state commanders," explained Wagner in 1944. "We cannot win the peace with forty-eight separate economic programs."

The health debate in the United States was starting to heat up. Further attention was focused during a US tour by William Beveridge in May of 1943, where he explained the plans for comprehensive health care in Britain in the form of the National Health Service. Beveridge's tour and his plans for social reform did not pass Roosevelt unnoticed. Although he had been unwilling to add health care to his Social Security Act in 1936 and world events had overtaken Wagner's bill in

1939, Roosevelt still considered himself the father of Social Security. Roosevelt resented Beveridge's growing status of social reformer and commented to an aide, "Why does Beveridge get his name on this? Why does he get the credit for this? You know that I have been talking about cradle-to-grave insurance ever since we first thought of it; it is my idea. It is not the Beveridge plan. It is the Roosevelt plan." Yet there was no Roosevelt plan.

Confronted by an expanded Republican presence in Congress and hindered by the Southern Democrats' fear of radical social programs, Roosevelt stalled. He was only too aware of the political power wielded by the AMA and the medical lobby. "We can't go up against the state medical societies. We just can't do it," he explained to Senator Walter George of the Senate Finance Committee. However, the president did submit his own ill-fated plans for national health care through the soon-to-be-defunct National Resource Planning Board, a vestige of the Depression era. When funding for the National Resources Planning Board was pulled by a hostile Congress, Roosevelt's plans died with him. Meanwhile, Roosevelt lent support to the Murray-Dingell bill, which he incorporated into his own plan in October of 1943, calling it the "American Plan." The American Plan proposed federal control of health care, but participation would be on a voluntary basis. Physicians and hospitals would remain independent and would be paid for their services at fixed rates. However, the increasingly hostile Congress never received the American Plan, and the conservative Democrats and Republicans made clear their opposition to health care reform.

Nonetheless, Wagner, Murray, and Dingell continued to advertise their plan for compulsory nationalized health care. In an opinion poll in 1944, 75 percent of Americans were in favor of a national health care plan. Alarmed by the increasing interest in "socialized medicine," the American Medical Association swung into action yet again. Referring to the planned Wagner bill, the AMA, through its *Journal of the American Medical Association*, commented, "It is doubtful if even Nazidom confers the powers which this measure would confer on the surgeon general of the US public health service." Supported by the pharmaceutical industry and hospital lobby, the AMA embarked on a massive press and radio campaign against "socialized medicine" and extolled the virtues of the free enterprise system that had made America "the healthiest nation in the world."

In November of 1944, Roosevelt was reelected to an unprecedented fourth term in office, and the ranks of his Republican and Democrat adversaries in Congress were thinned. He saw the opportunity for reintroducing plans for nationalized health care. A revised version of the Wagner, Murray, Dingell Bill was reintroduced, and in his State of the Union address in January of 1945, FDR promised "an expanded Social Security program, and adequate health and education programs." In the spring of 1945, the national health supporters were looking forward to congressional debate on health care in time for the troops returning from World War II, which was in its closing stages. However, for a third time, the health reform advocates were to be frustrated, this time by the death on April 12, 1945, of an ailing Franklin Roosevelt.

The health care issue was inherited by the prickly Missouri Democrat Harry Truman and was to prove one of his most disappointing legislative failures. Truman kept faith with Roosevelt's promise for a national health care plan and endorsed the Wagner, Murray, Dingell Bill, albeit in less than forceful terms. "I am not familiar with his details, but in principle, I am for it." Once accused of placing himself "dead center in the middle of stalemate," Truman lacked the political showmanship of his predecessor and, at times during the failed health care campaign, proved obstinate and uncompromising. The AMA was under no illusions about Truman's position on health care and soon swung into action against the thirty-third president. In November of 1945, Truman introduced his comprehensive national health care program, which called for comprehensive medical services for all workers and their dependents funded through the federal Social Security system.

After World War I, the worst and most prolonged period of Depression had settled over the United States. It was widely expected by the American public that history would repeat itself at the end of World War II. By 1946, however, the nation enjoyed economic prosperity and the safety net of expanded Social Security and massive government programs seemed unnecessary. An opinion poll asked the question, "What kind of health insurance would you prefer, government or private?" The nation was almost equally divided on the answer. Private health care insurance was dominated by Blue Cross, which covered hospital expenses, and Blue Shield plans, which covered physician expenses. The Blue Cross/Blue Shield plans were nonprofit, although commercial indemnity plans from insurance companies, such as The Prudential, commanded a corner of the market and a small revolutionary prepaid system, Kaiser Permanente, was its early years of existence.

The clamor for a nationalized plan showed signs of fading, and after the GOP takeover of Congress in November of 1946, the future of the Wagner, Murray, Dingell Bill was sealed, and the measure died in Congress. The reelection of Harry Truman in 1948 was a surprise to all and certainly a frustration to the American Medical Association. However, the political climate in America was changing and the antisocialist, anticommunist zeal was turning into hysteria. By labeling Truman's persistent calls for nationalized medicine as "socialized medicine," the AMA succeeded in riding the political tidal wave through America.

The AMA continued to campaign and advertise against Truman's federal plans for socialized medicine. In the midterm elections in 1950, the AMA embarked on a massive campaign labeled the National Education Campaign against Socialized Medicine. The AMA spent $2.25 million in 1950 campaigning against the "socializers in Washington" and "their compulsory medicine." Over a million dollars of this was spent during a two-week period leading up to the midterm congressional elections.

Other concerned interests, the insurance companies, the pharmaceutical industry, and the hospital lobby, produced "tie-in ads" that ran concurrently with the AMA blitz, to the tune of $2 million. Truman was encouraged by Dingell and other pro-administration lawmakers to chastise the AMA publicly for their increasingly hostile tactics. Once again, global events overtook Truman with the outbreak of hostilities on the Korean Peninsula in June of 1950. As the AMA press campaign was at its peak, the American public was distracted by reports of retreating US and NATO forces on the Korean Peninsula, pursued by communist forces. Truman was weakened. The Democrats, while retaining overall control of Congress, suffered a loss of five seats in the Senate and twenty-eight seats in the House. With the escalating war in Korea and a weakened Democratic presence in Congress, Truman's campaign for nationalized health care faded. The AMA found an ally in the new GOP president, Dwight Eisenhower, and his running mate, Richard Nixon, declaring there was "less danger of socialism than for a number of years."

The two-term Eisenhower administration soon realized that although private health insurance was burgeoning among the middle and upper classes, the poor and the aged remained out in the cold and unable to afford the premiums. The GOP's first plan was to provide federal money to expand the commercial and Blue Cross/Blue Shield plans while insulating them against any losses incurred. The plan was defeated by the Democrats, who balked at the concept of infusing government money into private companies.

The concept of nationalized compulsory health care was not a serious threat during the eight-year Eisenhower administration, and the AMA found themselves compromising on what would have previously been seen as threats. By the end of the Eisenhower administration, the AMA found itself supporting a Democrat plan sponsored by Senator Robert Kerr and Representative Wilbur Mills. The plan was a compromise between two opposing plans proposed during the 1960 presidential campaign. The GOP plan, sponsored by Senator Jarvis and endorsed by presidential hopeful, Richard Nixon, proposed federal funding of state health plans insuring the elderly and poor. Potential recipients were confined to those over the age of sixty-five, and recipients were means tested to evaluate eligibility.

The competing Democrat plan was sponsored by Representative Forand and championed by JFK in his presidential bid. The Democrat plan proposed federally funded health care for all Social Security recipients above the age of sixty-five, irrespective of income or assets. A compromise was struck: the Mills plan, which provided federal funding of state health plans for Americans above the age of sixty-five on a means-tested basis. The plan, which became known as "elderly disability," was endorsed by the AMA in an attempt to distract attention away from the more comprehensive Forand bill. A frustrated Senator Dingell, thwarted by the lack of any comprehensive national initiative, rationalized Eisenhower's disinterest by concluding that as a military man, he had been accustomed to "free socialized medicine" and was ignorant of the issues involved.

Medicare first entered the American vocabulary during the Eisenhower administration, although in a very different context from what it would eventually gain. Eisenhower's Medicare bill provided federal funds for hospital and physician services for veterans and their dependents. A few years later, the term would be "borrowed" by the Democratic Party as their flagship program for federal health care program. John F. Kennedy's election in 1960 convinced the health reformers that an overwhelming victory was within their grasp. The new president soon labeled his national health plan a priority, "must-do" legislation. The Democrats had also picked up thirty-two seats in the House of Representatives, and the Kennedy administration enjoyed a majority not seen in Congress since the Depression years.

In the early 1960s, the economy had been expanding at over 5 percent per year, and the economic prosperity provided a contented backdrop for liberal social reform. Kennedy's "New Frontier" agenda for health care was sponsored by Representative Cecil King from California and Senator Clinton

Anderson of New Mexico, both Democrats. Their plan was based on the Forand bill and called for federal funding of health care for all Americans over the age of sixty-five, irrespective of income and means. The plan was to be paid through Social Security. Representative Wilbur Mills of Arkansas, chairman of the House Ways and Means Committee and ranking Democrat, refused to consider the bill in the lower chamber. After Kennedy's assassination in November of 1963, however, attitudes on Capitol Hill underwent a metamorphosis. The assassination crystallized the upheaval absorbing America both at home and abroad. Violence was erupting on the streets in America as a result of the civil rights movement and an increasingly militant, antiwar movement. Abroad, America was embroiled in an escalating Vietnam War, and the Soviet threat appeared to be expanding, if not overtaking America.

Lyndon Johnson's landslide election in 1964 produced a further massive influx of liberal-minded Democrats into Congress, assuring passage of health care reform legislation. With fifty-eight new Democrats in the House and a greater presence on the House Ways and Means Committee, Chairman Wilbur Mills rethought his opposition and would reengineer health care plans to accommodate almost all parties. In the spring of 1965, the King-Anderson Bill, now known as "the Medicare Bill," was being debated in Congress. The AMA, staring defeat in the face, made one final bid to deflect the full impact of Medicare legislation. The AMA's "elder care," sponsored by conservative minorities in both houses, proposed expansion of federal funding to include doctor visits for those over sixty-five, albeit again on a means-tested basis. This measure, which was already covered under the Mills plan, seemed too little too late. "Bettercare" was sponsored by Representative John Byrnes of Wisconsin, a Republican. The Byrnes bill offered a comprehensive health care plan for all Social Security recipients. The plan was to be voluntary and would be paid for by a monthly three-dollar deduction from their Social Security checks.

Wilbur Mills, who by now had shifted direction 180 degrees, incorporated elements from the AMA's plan and the Republican minority's plan and added these provisions to the Democrats' Medicare proposals. The plan emerging from the House Ways and Means Committee, renamed the Mills Plan, included hospital insurance for all Americans over sixty-five (the King-Anderson Plan), a voluntary plan to cover physician fees for a three-dollar-charge from Social Security benefits (the Republican plan), and federal funding of state-run health insurance for the indigent (the AMA plan). The King-Anderson provisions would be known as Medicare A, to pay for hospital costs. The Republican plan for voluntary contributions for physician costs would become Medicare B. The AMA's proposals, expanding the existing care, Mills' program, would become Medicaid. On July 27, 1965, the House passed the Medicare bill on a vote of 307 to 116. The following day, the Senate voted the measure into law by a majority of seventy to twenty-four. Two days later, on July 20, 1965, Lyndon Johnson traveled down to Independence, Missouri, where he signed Medicare, Title XVIII of the Social Security Act, and Medicaid, Title XIX of the Social Security Act, into law. Harry Truman, now confined to a wheelchair, sat next to the president and accepted four of the pens used to sign the measure into law.

American's campaign for a comprehensive nationalized health care system had started during the Great Depression and had taken over thirty years to bear fruit. Even then, the plan included only the elderly and the needy, falling far short of the universal and comprehensive plan introduced in Britain almost twenty years earlier. July 30, 1965, was the high-water mark for nationalized medicine in the United States. Health care costs were already escalating. In the 1950s, they had doubled, and during the first half of the 1960s, they had doubled again. The opening of the federal purse to the seemingly insatiable appetites of health care would add fuel to the flames. Within six weeks of signing the Medicare legislation, Lyndon Johnson ordered congressional hearings into soaring health care prices. Federal funds for Medicare and Medicaid were not fixed budgets, as were Treasury allocations to the National Health Service. The cost of the programs was directly proportional to the utilization, and escalating costs was a self-fulfilling prophecy. For the next three and a half decades, health care reform would not focus on expanding and increasing eligibility and services but would turn each sinew of its strength into reining in health care expenditures.

In the early 1960s, medical inflation was 3.2 percent a year, and Medicare grew more than 7.9 percent annually. Per capita health costs rose from $142 in 1960 to $198 in 1965. By 1970, the figure was $336. Hospital costs increased 8 percent annually during the 1950s, and after 1965, the rate of growth was 14 percent annually. In 1965, the federal government spent $10.8 billion on health care. Five years later, this figure was $27.8 billion. Richard Nixon, who inherited medical inflation in 1968, sought to curb its expansion while Senator Edward Kennedy sought to liberalize medical care in the form of a single, federally operated health insurance system.

The Nixon administration explored and instituted a new concept in health care, the health maintenance organization. In the late 1960s and early 1970s, a Minneapolis physician,

Paul M. Ellwood, was voicing his concept for structural reform within the health care industry. Ellwood proposed reorganizing the health care industry to shift from a fee-for-service system, which encouraged long hospital stays and multiple procedures, to a prepayment system for comprehensive health care, which was fixed irrespective of the number of interventions performed or length of stay.

Ellwood's HMO concept was not new, since plans such as the Kaiser plan had been in existence since World War II. The health maintenance strategy made sense to the Nixon administration, and HMO plans were introduced under Medicare and Medicaid in an attempt to curtail escalating costs. In February of 1971, Nixon announced his new national health strategy, which used HMOs as the primary instrument of his plans. Citing the "illogical incentives" inherent in fee-for-service plans, Nixon requested $45 million in grants to set up new HMOs. Within twelve months, thirty HMOs were in operation with plans to subsidize the creation of up to two thousand HMOs that would serve the vast majority of the American people. The AMA, wounded over the Medicare battles, predictably resisted the HMO concept and, instead, proposed tax relief on premiums for private health care insurance.

Several schemes were proposed to curb runaway medical inflation: One such scheme to curtail Medicare costs was suggested in the form of the professional standards review organization (PRSO), which oversaw utilization of Medicare and Medicaid resources. These independent organizations would regulate utilization of Medicare resources, denying inappropriate procedures, unnecessary admissions, and lengthy hospital stays. The medical lobby countered with a demand for physicians to sit on the PRSOs, thus protecting themselves from lay control. Referred to by critics as "the fox looking after the henhouse," the controversial PSRO was never effective and was found to cost more to administer than it actually saved.

In spite of these initiatives, health care costs in the mid-1970s continued to surge. Price regulations were implemented in the form of wage and price freezes. When the wage and price freezes were relaxed in 1973, they remained in force for doctor fees, capped at 2.5 percent, and annual increases in hospital charges, which were pegged at 6 percent. After Nixon's reelection in 1972, the administration bowed to growing public opinion and opposition pressure (chiefly from Senator Edward Kennedy) and announced plans for a national insurance plan. The plan, relying heavily on the HMO concept, used private insurance companies to provide coverage for the employed. The unemployed would be covered under a separate government program. Patients would be required to pay 25 percent of their medical bills up to a maximum of $1,500 a year.

Kennedy, who had softened his original plan for a comprehensive federal insurance plan, now proposed using the private sector as a fiscal intermediary. Under the Kennedy plan, patients would be responsible for 25 percent copayments, with an annual cap of $1,000 per individual. By June of 1974, the administration and the Democrats were approaching reconciliation. "A spirit of compromise is in the air," expounded Senator Kennedy that summer. The concept of a Republican president proposing a nationalized health plan, against the recommendations of his entire cabinet, was a new and unexpected tactic in the forty-year health care war. However, 1974 was the year of Watergate, and Nixon's motives in proposing such federal largesse have been questioned.

Had it not been for Watergate, the Nixon program may have been radically different. In practice, the plans were scotched when Nixon resigned. In spite of a large Democratic majority in Congress, the campaign for nationalized health insurance plan was soon dropped by President Ford.

Frustrated over President Jimmy Carter's lack of progress in the health care theater, Edward Kennedy proposed his third version of a national health care system. Under Kennedy's third plan for nationalized health system, the private sector would be the engine of reform, with HMOs as the pivotal strategy. Employed Americans would be offered a range of health care plans with low-cost HMOs playing a leading role. Competition among health plans would keep down health care premiums as consumers sought the maximum range of benefits for the least-expensive premium. Employers would pay 65 percent of the health care premiums and consumers 35 percent. The unemployed and uninsured would be covered by a government plan yet to be devised. This would be paid for through payroll taxes. Americans covered through the private sector and through the government plan would have indistinguishable health care cards, to prevent bias or preference among providers. The whole system would be overseen by government departments and subject to budget constraints.

Kennedy's plan never reached Congress. The growing rift between Kennedy and Carter made more headlines than health care reform. Additionally, health care reform yet again took a back seat to world developments. In 1979, American hostages had been taken in Tehran, and for 444 days, the public would be distracted nightly by images of blindfolded and bound hostages led to captivity. The standoff climaxed with a failed rescue attempt by the US Marines, followed by a live TV acceptance of responsibility by Carter himself, compounding the humiliation for his administration. This was not a political atmosphere for any initiative, far less, radical and contentious health care reform. Kennedy's health care plan never reached Congress. However, it would be resurrected twenty years later under a new name but with remarkable similarities to its predecessor. The Clinton health care plan called for almost identical provisions as the Kennedy plan, but this time, employers would foot 80 percent of the costs.

When Jimmy Carter left office in 1980, eight million Americans, 4 percent of the population, were enrolled in HMO plans. This was twice the number from ten years previously; however, it fell far short of the 90 percent enrollment predicted by the Nixon Administration in 1973. The system appeared to be top heavy and overburdened by a long list of professional review bodies and federal regulatory agencies. The PRSO, a professional regulatory body designed to review and contain escalating health care costs, was found to cost more than it actually saved. Other Nixon-era regulations, such as the hospital certificate of need (CON) program, designed to slow the growth in hospital beds, faced severe restrictions: The CON program had no jurisdiction over freestanding surgical centers, and diagnostic facilities such as MRI and CT scan centers and single specialty clinics were exempt. Utilization flourished, and health inflation soared.

When Ronald Reagan was elected in 1980, gone was the bureaucratic control of the Nixon era and the social idealism of the Carter administration. Government regulatory bodies such as the PRSOs, HSAs, and other Nixon-era agencies were disbanded. Under Ronald Reagan, the free market would prevail.

Chapter 6

THE BATTLE OF BRIDGEPORT

IN 1985, HAVING DECIDED TO STAY PERMANENTLY IN THE United States, I negotiated a residency post in the Yale University surgical program in neighboring Bridgeport, Connecticut. I arrived late on a summer evening on a Saturday night at Bridgeport Hospital and encountered another surgical resident, who would be one of my colleagues for the next few years. Finding our way around the area, unfamiliar to both of us, we made our way toward a somewhat-dilapidated barracks-like building located behind the hospital, which would be the temporary residence for the new surgical residents. In the fading light, we struggled to open the locked door in front of the barracks hut, with the provided key. Suddenly, a bullet stuck the doorframe above our heads and ricocheted into the night air. I have never been shot at before in my life; however, I needed no explanation as to what had just happened. We ducked and ran out of the area, to return later.

Returning after dark, we managed to enter the building without further incident. Although I was not shot at again, to my knowledge, dealing with gunshot wounds would be a huge part of my role as a surgical resident in a major urban hospital within reach of the New York drug frenzy.

In the 1980s, the city of Bridgeport had fallen on hard times. Once called the "Park City," downtown Bridgeport had degraded into a war zone between competing drug gangs. On weekend-call evenings, a few of the on-call residents would stand on the roof of the eight-story Bridgeport Hospital and gaze toward downtown Bridgeport. The crackle of automatic fire from the drug wars was a constant feature, and we christened this "the Battle of Bridgeport." Located on the fringe of New York City in the 1980s' drug-induced frenzy of murder and mayhem, and prior to Rudolph Giuliani's clean-up of gangs and drugs, Bridgeport was a commuter community for violent criminals. We witnessed the first Teflon-coated bullets, which the media christened "cop killers." On one random Saturday night, a shot-up police car limped into the entrance to the emergency room; the occupants were ushered in to be treated. "My God," the injured police officer exclaimed. "Now they have bazookas!"

In spite of working for several years in the emergency room in Edinburgh, I had never seen a single gunshot wound. The first day of covering the emergency room, there were no less than three gunshot wounds awaiting my attention. All of these three were gunshots to the lower limbs, which I was told were warning shots from drug dealers to caution their customers about late payments. The next shot would be in the chest or abdomen if they were to default again on their payments. The violence resulting from the drug crisis in Bridgeport was gratuitous and grotesque. On one random, hot summer night, a semi-conscious, middle-aged black male was dropped off (literally) at the ER entrance, from an urban taxi (aka, a stolen car), which, without even slowing down, sped off anonymously into the night. With an astonished audience of onlookers, we quickly stabilized his cervical spine (neck) and threw him unceremoniously onto a stretcher and rushed him into the Trauma Room. There, we all stared uncomprehendingly at an eight-inch piece of firewood protruding from his right eye, embedded into the frontal lobe of his brain. Rather naively, I asked him what had happened, and he told me he had been hit in the eye with a pool cue. This rough piece of firewood was certainly no pool cue, and the end of the wood still bore the hammer marks used to hammer the wood through the victim's eye, through his skull, and into the frontal lobe of his brain. Remarkably, after several hours in the operating room, the wood stake was removed, and after several weeks of repeat surgeries and a long rehabilitation, he left the hospital alive, albeit blind in his right eye, but reasonably functional.

A year later, a professional assassin came to Bridgeport to settle some outstanding scores. The modus operandi of this particular assassin was to shoot his victims from behind, through the back of the neck, through the lower cervical spine (lower neck, around C7), just high enough to ensure these victims would be quadriplegic for the rest of their days, condemned to laying on their backs and staring at the ceiling. The shot was placed with such accuracy that it was delivered just below the breathing center, which was essential for these patients to remain breathing. During the next year, there were three victims of this assassin, lying forever on their backs, on ventilators, with identical gunshots in the backs of their necks.

The Columbian gangs had a different calling card. Their weapon of choice was the chainsaw, which was used to amputate the forearms of their victims. The Scots, I soon realized, had a lot to learn from these guys.

Compared to Britain, US hospitals were remarkably modern and well equipped. This was the first time in my career that I was working in a hospital that was less than a hundred years old. Even the mundane tasks of drawing blood, sending it to the lab, inserting IV cannulas for IV access, and inserting nasogastric tubes were performed by teams of phlebotomists, IV-access teams, and well-trained nurses. Blunt trauma to the abdomen or gunshots were wheeled immediately to the CT scanners. Even elective, routine scans were performed within twenty-four hours, rather than the one- to two-week wait I was accustomed to back home. The MRI, a recent American-British invention, was freely available in the United States and was not even in routine use back in Britain. The PET scanner (this time, a wholly US invention) identified metastasis (spread) of cancer throughout the body.

The decision to stay was an easy one. In the United States, surgical residencies are typically five years and are organized to include all the specialties and subspecialties required to train a competent and safe surgeon. After the five-year residency, the graduating chief residents are free to enter private practice, wherever in the United States they chose to live and work. This was a fluid, versatile, free market system, and nobody was waiting for dead man's shoes. Any new surgical graduate was free to start his or her new career in any state (subject to state licensure) and apply and enter any hospital or practice in the United States (subject to the usual thorough vetting and credentialing process) without any quota or limit on physician staffing.

The efficiency of a free market health care system was refreshing compared to a government-run operation. Surgeons in private practice are only too happy to operate on the private patients the next day, if appropriate, rather than put their names on waiting lists. It is immaterial whether the case starts at 7:00 a.m. or 7:00 p.m. Although subject to availability in the operating room, the number of operating rooms available around the clock allowed for a very thorough and efficient output of patients, rather than adding their names to the waiting lists. Medicine in the United States is a business, and business rules apply.

The majority of US hospitals, approximately 75 percent, are not-for-profit institutions. The not-for-profit status does not mean in any way shape or form that these hospitals do not generate significant income and, indeed, profit. The not-for-profit status is a legal status wherein hospitals are not subject to property tax or revenue tax, in exchange for treating the uninsured or indigent of the community. Any profits that are made are used for capital purchases for the hospital or to improve or expand their facilities. Added to this, charitable donations and corporate philanthropy add to the coffers. If a not-for-profit hospital requires capital, it enters the municipal bond market, where capital can be generated and interest rates for the loans are determined by the hospital's credit rating. A good credit rating means a low interest rate on their loan; a poor credit rating means a high interest or no loan whatsoever. The for-profit hospitals pay property taxes and revenue taxes, and if capital is needed, they approach their shareholders. For-profit hospitals answer to the shareholders at the end of the day but must still deliver quality care to their patients or risk insolvency and loss of share price, the same as any other business operation. Government and state hospitals are typically large, urban hospitals in underfunded and underserved areas, and funded by local taxpayers. These hospitals inevitably have a higher proportion of indigent and uninsured individuals, a burden the local county taxpayers accept, albeit reluctantly in many or most cases. In spite of the greater efficiency in delivering medicine, the readier access to up-to-date equipment, and the freedom to operate whenever was convenient for all concerned, there were a few drawbacks. In private practice, I paid $75,000 per year for medical malpractice coverage. I certainly missed my fifty-dollar contribution to the Medical Defense Union, which was paid annually in Britain for malpractice coverage.

In order to ensure efficiency, high quality, and effectiveness, teams of individuals in US hospitals monitored all surgical patients and even the surgeons themselves. The length of stay was carefully monitored by utilization review. The patient's eligibility for care in the hospital was determined by a precertification team to ensure the procedure was warranted and the hospital was paid. If the procedure was deemed unwarranted or not covered by the plan, the patient would be faced with an unwelcome and unexpected bill for their experience and be faced with the need to pay out of pocket.

Surgical outcomes were monitored by a small army of performance improvement (PI) specialists, who tracked outcomes and, more specifically, examined why complications had occurred. Each patient was typically assigned a case manager, typically answerable to the insurance company, to ensure they were discharged from the hospital in a timely manner rather than dwell in the hospital a day or two longer than necessary.

This new environment of health care delivery and surgical practice was a refreshing change from Britain. The pay-for-service model, widely criticized by health care analysts as a vehicle for health care inflation, ensured that the American public received their health care in a timely manner in modern facilities and with good outcomes. Whatever drawbacks the pay-for-service model may have, it certainly delivered efficiency where efficiency was demanded and quality where quality was not negotiable.

The contrast between the National Health Service and the United States came sharply into focus during a visit to a long-term health care facility, harshly nicknamed "ventilator farms," where patients with little or no hope of survival, typically unconscious, remaining on ventilators for weeks, months, and sometimes even years. This was the first time I had entered such a facility. I was shocked and was immediately reminded of the movie *Coma*. I walked through wards lined with patients lying on beds, unconscious or sedated, on ventilators, and provided with every last intervention that modern medicine could deliver to keep them alive, often for the sake of keeping them alive. Typically grieving relatives, reluctant or unable to withdraw care (lacking the necessary power of attorney), were forced to allow these individuals to live in the no-man's-land between life and death, suspended for prolonged periods of a vegetative state without hope of regaining consciousness or even survival. It struck me that it was a very bitter irony from health care delivery in the National Health Service, where those who were deserving of care, with a decent chance of survival, were not offered it. In contrast, in the United States, those unfortunate individuals, who were faced with no hope of survival, were provided every last vestige of care, often to no point or purpose whatsoever.

Chapter 7

THE RISE AND FALL OF THE HMO

PRIOR TO THE AFFORDABLE CARE ACT, NO SINGLE development in the health arena has had as dramatic an impact on the delivery of health care, or caused such controversy and debate, as the HMO. Conceived and created by Paul Ellwood in the late 1960s, the concept of the HMO was, in theory, to provide an answer to escalating health care costs. The principle involved prepayment of regular fixed monthly premiums to providers, both physicians and hospitals, in return for unlimited and unrestricted care for the plan enrollees. This removed the incentive for physicians to "over treat" their patient by performing unnecessary procedures, or hospitals to prolong inpatient stays, as was the perceived problem with the traditional fee-for-service plans. By shifting the health care from a fee-for-service basis to prepaid plans, overutilization would be discouraged, and the runaway health care inflation would be reined in.

Although the concept sounded logical in principle and rational in design, it went far beyond the limits of constraint and became a byword for denial, obstruction, and neglect. The name itself, health maintenance organization, portrayed the concept of providing low-cost preventive measures to a wide population, thereby maintaining their health and, theoretically, preventing disease. Although the financial basis for HMOs made economic sense, the conceptual basis of the system was at best naïve and at worst (and there would be many examples of the very worst) bureaucratic obstruction and organized denial.

Paul Ellwood, a rehabilitation specialist, was well versed in the principles of disease prevention by such procedures as immunizations and population screening for carcinoma, and the health benefits of such programs as smoking cessation and weight loss. However, even the most rudimentary understanding of medicine or social behavior should have made it obvious that such well-intentioned plans would not halt the relentless progression of most lethal conditions. Not all diseases are preventable. Nor would the most strident prevention programs eradicate the huge reservoir of existing diseases, which require treatment, not prevention. Sooner or later, everyone, without exception, will develop a serious and life-threatening condition. Sooner or later, that condition will ordinarily require potentially expensive diagnosis and even more costly intervention in the form of surgery or medication. The HMO concept itself was relying on a lifelong state of benign coexistence with the health plan, preferably followed by a sudden and unexpected death. The term "health maintenance organization" itself was, therefore, a misnomer and a flawed concept from the outset. The most troubling concern is how health care intellectuals, planners, and pundits took twenty-five years to arrive at this seemingly obvious conclusion.

Prepaid health plans, the progenitor of the HMO industry, can be traced back to the Great Depression. One of its first pioneers was a young surgeon, Sidney R. Garfield, who found himself in charge of a twelve-bed hospital in the middle of the Mojave Desert in the 1930s. His patient population consisted of several thousand construction workers building the Los Angeles Aqueduct. Finding himself without adequate facilities to treat such a large population base, without the ability to transfer to a larger center, the ambitious Dr. Garfield borrowed money to build Contractors General Hospital. Burdened by loans to repay capital costs and without a steady income, he soon found himself in financial straits. The surgeon turned to Harold Hatch, an engineer turned insurance broker, who persuaded the construction companies to pay Dr. Garfield a small per diem rate for each of their workers, to cover any anticipated health care needs that may be necessary. For five cents a day, each worker was eligible for treatment of work-related injuries, and for a further five cents per day, non-work-related conditions would be treated. With thousands of enrollees, Dr. Garfield and Contractors General Hospital were soon flush with cash.

With the completion of the Los Angeles Aqueduct, Garfield moved to another massive construction project, this time, the Grand Coulee Dam, which was managed by industrialist, Henry Kaiser. Here, Garfield employed the same prepaid health care system that had proven so successful on the Los Angeles Aqueduct project. The success did not go unnoticed by Henry Kaiser, who saw the potential of introducing the concept into the Kaiser shipyards in Richmond, California. As the United States was embarking on a massive armaments program, on the eve of their entry into World War II, in 1941, the Kaiser shipyards employed 30,000 workers building Liberty ships and aircraft carriers for the war effort. Having received a personal release from military service by President Franklin

Roosevelt, Dr. Garfield moved to the Richmond shipyards, where his patient base reached almost 100,000 by the end of the war. At war's end, Kaiser opened the Kaiser Permanente Health Plan to the public, where its membership tripled to over 300,000 in the first ten years. Backed by the support of organized labor, including the International Longshoremen & Warehousemen's Union, the plan spread from northern California along the West Coast.

Although Dr. Garfield found a place in history with his successful prepaid health plans, this did not occur without a significant element of good luck. By providing health care to a relatively young and healthy workforce, Garfield avoided the millstone of most health plans in the form of elderly patients, with chronic and longstanding health problems. Another significant plus was the fact that all his patients were employed and had the means to subscribe to his plan in the first place. Fortune also smiled on Garfield by making him the only physician in the middle of the Mojave Desert. With a young and healthy patient base, all of whom were fully employed and able to contribute, and by avoiding any competition, it is hard to imagine how Garfield's health plan could possibly have failed.

Insurance industries the world over owed their existence to avoiding high-risk exposures and accumulating low-risk enrollees. This principle underlies both the for-profit and not-for-profit insurance world. The flagship of the not-for-profit health plans, Blue Cross/Blue Shield, found its origins, like Kaiser, in the Depression era.

In 1929, Justin Ford Kimball was faced with the task of reversing the financial decline of Baylor University Hospital in Dallas, Texas. Kimball, an accountant by trade, calculated the per diem cost of providing a hospital bed and, having added a profit margin, offered a fixed-budget health plan to fifteen hundred local school teachers. The plan provided up to twenty-one days of hospital care for a fixed cost of six dollars per person. Kimball's insurance plan caught on, and the prepaid, fixed-cost hospital insurance plan evolved to become the Blue Cross plan, which spread from state to state to become the largest such plan in the nation. While Kimball concentrated on prepaid hospital care, a similar plan for physician coverage, or the Blue Shield plan, grew out of the lumber and mining camps of the Pacific Northwest in the early 1900s. Lumber companies, which traditionally have high injury rates, approached local physicians to create an insurance plan to cover their workers in the event of with accidents and injuries. The first Blue Shield plan, organized in Tacoma, Washington, in 1917, gave birth to a quickly evolving network of health plans to provide insurance to pay for physician's services. Blue Cross and Blue Shield merged in 1982 as one of the largest nonprofit health care plans.

As indemnity plans, premium rates for such plans were calculated on a retrospective basis for the community covered, setting "community rates" for policy premiums. With time, smaller for-profit insurance corporations soon entered into the marketplace and selected out groups of low-risk individuals to whom they offered less expensive rates. By avoiding high-risk individuals, they were soon able to undercut the competition. As the marketplace matured, and competition stiffened, even nonprofit companies such as Blue Cross/Blue Shield adopted experience rating as a basis for pricing health policies. In the latter half of the twentieth century, life expectancy in the US reached the eighties, nineties, and beyond. As new invasive procedures evolved and previously fatal disease became treatable, death was averted, but at the same time, the sick became sicker and required longer hospital stays. The sicker people became, the more procedures were required, and the longer they lived. It was a self-perpetuating system. The number and complexity of medical procedures performed underwent exponential growth, and the stage was set for an explosion in insurance premiums that would impact both the for-profit and not-for-profit sectors alike.

By the late 1970s and early 1980s, runaway health inflation followed by financial recession led many corporations, including leading Fortune 500 companies, to eliminate the insurance middleman and to self-insure against their employees' medical costs. This made the corporations themselves directly responsible for their employees' medical bills, from the first dollar onward, rather than insure against such events. Having now assumed the financial risk of their employees' ill health, they were astonished at the size of the hospital bill for simple procedures. As a cushion against potentially massive debt from medical bills, corporations increasingly shifted the financial burden to the employees themselves, by adding annual deductibles and copays for procedures, hospital stays, and even doctor visits. Increasingly, employees were faced with increasing annual deductibles transferring the "first-dollar" costs to the health consumers themselves. Copayments of 20 percent, sometimes higher, for surgical procedures helped insulate employers from the full impact of health care costs and acted as a deterrent to workers seeking medical attention. This proved a temporizing measure, however, and the fee-for-service strategy of health care proved to be a more systemic problem requiring major surgery.

Well-publicized examples of the day-to-day impact of health care costs on corporate America provided some sobering examples. In the 1980s, for instance, General Motors paid more for health care for its employees than it paid for steel to manufacture motor cars. In a 1991 *Fortune* magazine article, Goodyear's CEO calculated the company needed to manufacture 42 radial tires to pay for one appendectomy. Budweiser's CEO calculated it needed to sell 1,627 six-packs of twelve ounce Budweiser to pay for the same procedure. George Ander's book *"Health against Wealth"* quotes the most colorful example, from Dayton-Hudson retailers in Minneapolis, who calculated they had to sell 39,000 Ninja Turtles to pay for the same appendectomy. Faced with these startling realities, the coming of the HMO appeared to be in the nick of time.

In the 1980s, in spite of the success of the Kaiser plan, prepaid health plans remained out of the health insurance mainstream. They were widely regarded (incorrectly) as cut-price plans providing what must, therefore, be a second-rate service. The public (decades before the pundits) could not fathom how they could deliver the same quality of care as mainstream indemnity insurance plans but for a much lower premium. The prepaid plans, now bearing the more respectable title of HMOs, received a significant boost in their images during Nixon's campaign for health care reform. Seen as a logical method of reining in double-digit health care costs, the HMO industry received the federal seal of approval. Nixon's campaign culminated in the HMO Act of 1973, which required firms employing more than twenty-five employees to offer an HMO plan as an option to their employees. Congress approved $375 million over five years to finance the start-up of the HMO industry. The Nixon administration forecast that over 63 million Americans would be enrolled in an HMO by the end of the decade. In reality, by 1985, less than 18 million had enrolled. Although the HMO Act did not dramatically influence health care delivery in its early years, the act did provide an air of legitimacy to the plans and gave them a significant boost in prestige and availability.

The downturn in the economy in the 1980s, rampant inflation, and runaway medical costs provided fertile ground in which HMOs would flourish. In the early 1980s, America's largest corporations hit hard financial times. The CEOs of the largest corporations looked to their ledgers in search of cost savings. They did not have to look far. Such large employers such as Allied Signal, Digital Equipment Corporation, GTE Corporation, AT&T, and Xerox embraced the fledgling HMO companies in the hopes of controlling massive and expanding health care costs. Smaller employers banded together to form purchasing corporations with the ability to negotiate lower rates from the HMOs. Previously unknown HMOs were soon seen as the potential saviors of American's struggling corporations. Fledgling companies such as Humana, U.S. Healthcare, UnitedHealthcare, and WellPoint competed fiercely with the established East Coast indemnity insurers such as Aetna, Cigna, Travelers, and Metropolitan Life.

The second great boost to the HMO industry came in the debate leading to the 1992 presidential election when Democratic hopeful Bill Clinton made health care reform a cornerstone of his presidential campaign. The Clinton health care proposal, like many before and after, frequently lacked specifics and was especially vague on financing. However, the principal of universal health care for all Americans remained at the center of his campaign. Recognizing the potential of the

HMO to curb as-yet-untamed medical inflation, and having little allegiance to the medical profession, Clinton made the HMO the centerpiece of his health plan. The phrase "managed competition within a budget" was the war cry of the HMO pundits and was predicted to revolutionize America's health care delivery. "Managed competition" was a concept introduced by Alain Enthoven, a Stanford University health care economist. Enthoven had spent the 1960s as Assistant Secretary of Defense during the Vietnam War. After the war, seeking a change in profession, he developed an interest in health care delivery. An adept politician, he became the director of Georgetown University and was, later, an advisor to the Carter administration to assist in their efforts on health care reform. Enthoven proposed the concept of managed competition, a parallel theme to managed care, and this caught the eye of the Clinton campaign effort.

Managed competition had two principles. First, the availability of several HMO plans would stimulate competition between plans, thus driving down health care premiums and increasing the range of benefits offered. Employees would be free to choose among a number of differing health plans, including traditional indemnity plans and the increasingly competitive HMOs. The second great pillar of managed competition focused on the consumer. Health care premiums on the consumer side would be driven down by encouraging employees to choose the lower-cost HMO option, rather than the more expensive indemnity plans. This was achieved by implementing a series of tax incentives for enrolling in low-cost HMO plans and disincentives against selecting the higher-cost indemnity plans. The cutoff point for the tax threshold was placed sufficiently low to persuade most employees to enroll in an HMO. If individuals insisted on opting for the more traditional indemnity plans, not only was this more expensive, but also the increment was not tax deductible.

To save out-of-pocket expenses, people flocked to the HMOs. Such tax incentives were not new in the health care market. The federal government employed such a plan in the Federal Employees Health Benefits Program, which had been in existence since the late 1950s. The Clinton health plan would be a highly regulated system and subjective to budget constraints. A health care czar would oversee the program, and the entire health care industry would be brought under the heavy hand of the federal government. Uninsured individuals would be covered under a federally sponsored plan providing the same basic package as those in the private sector. The plan was Kennedy 3.0 from 1970.

Ironically, the failure of the Clinton health plan was a shot in the arm for the HMO industry. Although they had been lauded as the means of fiscal restraint in the Clinton health plan, the HMOs had also faced the specter of federal regulation and tight budget constraints. Conceived during the presidential campaign, and facing intense political and growing public disdain during the first two years of the new Clinton administration, the Clinton health plan died. With the collapse of Clinton's health care reform, the HMOs had escaped incarceration on Pennsylvania Avenue. Almost overnight, they headed, instead, to Wall Street.

Since the 1960s, most HMOs had been nonprofit, tax-exempt organizations. The executives were paid modest salaries, and the fledgling organizations were widely regarded as unpretentious and dutifully plowed back any profits into improving patient care. During the late 1980s, as HMOs grew in size and prestige, many saw the obvious benefits of changing their status to for-profit. The greatest incentive to this turnaround in philosophy was a massive injection of capital from the issue of publicly traded stocks. Overnight the philosophy of the entire organization changed from one of being responsible for their patients to being held responsible by the stockholders. This dramatic shift in philosophy would come back to haunt the HMO industry in the decades to come, but not before many of its CEOs retired as multimillionaires. In 1960, most of the fledgling HMOs were not-for-profit. By 1990, 33 percent of HMOs had changed their statuses to for-profit. By 1995, after the failed Clinton health reform, 50 percent had changed their statuses to for-profit. By 1998, this figure would exceed 80 percent. Having changed their statuses to for-profit, the HMOs shifted their attentions from charting their patients' progress to charting their stocks' prices. Investors flocked to the new HMOs, believing that having successfully cut expenditures by slashing provider fees, a healthy chunk of premiums from the expanding patient base could be disbursed as profits.

In the first half of the 1990s, the stock price of most publicly traded HMOs revealed a very healthy picture, with the price increasing almost unstoppably as patients flooded from the expensive indemnity plans to enroll in the new HMOs. With a healthy bottom line, surging stock values, and bloating market capitalization, the CEOs could now demand bonus salaries and stock options hitherto unheard of. David A. Jones, cofounder of Kentucky-based Humana, turned a thousand-dollar investment in a small nursing home (Heritage House in Louisville, Kentucky) into a $200 million personal fortune by 1994. Leonard Abramson, founder of US Healthcare, turned $16,000 of his personal savings in 1976 into a $1 billion personal fortune twenty years later. With a $3.5 million annual salary and $11 million dividend income in 1976, the HMO tycoon was the idol of his fellow CEOs. Following the same path as the Vanderbilts, Rockefellers, Hearsts, and Gates of America, Leonard Abramson simply found himself in the right place at the right time. For the HMO industry, the early 1990s were certainly the right times.

Having been given a mandate to rein in the incomes of physicians and other health care providers, the frequent excesses displayed by the CEOs of the increasingly powerful HMO industry provided a case lesson in double standards. More seriously, the philosophy of denial was reducing America's access to health care. By this "double denial" to both providers and patients alike, the HMOs soon lost popularity. The heyday of the HMO industry from 1990 until 1995 saw an almost linear growth in the number of Americans covered by some form of managed care plan. According to a study by the Henry J. Kaiser Family Foundation, a health care think tank, 225 million Americans had some form of health insurance in 1997. Of these over half, 127 million were enrolled in some form of managed care plan. This period also saw an almost parallel growth in the proportion of for-profit HMOs, reaching in excess of 60 percent of the managed care industry by 1998. Because of a frenzy of mergers and acquisitions, this period saw no increase in the actual number of HMOs, which remained relatively stable around six hundred. As enrollment continued to swell and the stock price of the for-profit HMOs continued its climb, merger mania hit the industry.

The largest of these mergers involved the unlikely marriages between traditional East Coast indemnity insurance plans, such as Aetna and Prudential, with some of the most precocious

HMOs, such as Humana and US Healthcare. Recognizing the obvious success of the HMO strategy, traditional insurance providers sought new markets by copying the tactics of the upstart managed care companies. The new HMO industry also relied extensively on sophisticated information technology that kept careful track of activities of both patients and providers alike. An enormous computer database micromanaged control of patient access to physicians and dictated the denial or authorization of diagnostic tests or surgical procedures. An entire culture grew out of the process of curtailing doctor visits, denying surgical procedures, and curtailing hospital stays, a whole industry unto itself, known as "utilization review." For this, the HMOs had sophisticated computer networks to monitor, regulate, and control every step of the process, beginning before the patient stepped into the doctor's office and ending after they stepped out of the hospital lobby. Failure to recognize the importance of this massive database, or to neglect these sophisticated computer networks, could unravel the entire corporation. Oxford Health Plans was to find out this simple fact to their massive cost in 1997 when their computer system "blew a fuse," making them impotent to direct patients or providers and causing their stock to lose 80 percent of its value overnight.

The most successful HMOs boasted the most successful information technology systems. This made them attractive takeover targets for the established insurance companies. Frequently, however, the roles of the established East Coast insurance companies and the precocious HMOs were reversed: now, the old insurers played the role of blushing bride. In 1994, Travelers Insurance Company and Metropolitan Life Insurance Company found themselves left behind in the new health care stakes and combined their struggling operations to form Metrahealth. The following year, Minneapolis-based UnitedHealthcare Corporation, founded by Paul Ellwood himself, purchased Metrahealth for $1.65 billion in one of the largest and hitherto unthinkable ironies of the new health care market. In April of 1996, Aetna purchased Pennsylvania-based US Healthcare for a massive $8.8 billion dollars. By adding 2.8 million new enrollees, the purchase represented a price tag of over $3,000 per head for each new enrollee. Two years later, Aetna assimilated NYLCare Health Plans for a further $1.05 billion dollars. With 2.2 million new enrollees, or a price tag of $477 per head, it was becoming clear that the giant's appetite for high-priced acquisitions was mellowing. Nonetheless, in December of that same year, Aetna announced another $1 billion acquisition, this time acquiring Prudential HealthCare. With 6.6 million enrollees, this represented bargain basement enrollees of only $151 per head.

The wave of mergers and the frenzy of consolidation led to speculation of a new handful of megacorporations dominating the health care industry in the United States. Solomon Brothers projected that the new millennium would contain no more than five or six national HMO companies. The tidal wave of mergers among HMOs drew concern from health care analysts. Slashing provider fees, restricting access to providers, and the much-vaunted economies of scale were not translating into lower premiums.

In 1997, the cost-curve reversed course and took a dramatic upturn, as managed-care premiums started to climb again after a brief hiatus of relatively stable costs. Other megamergers of the era included WellPoint Health Networks, a for-profit creation of Blue Cross of California. In 1996, the fledgling plan purchased the health care business of Massachusetts Mutual

Life Company for $380 million, followed in short order by the purchase of John Hancock Mutual Life Insurance Company, for $86.7 million. These mergers were intended to allow the HMOs to increase their presence in hitherto untapped markets. By purchasing Metro Health, United Healthcare was able to grow from an established presence in the Midwest and East Coast to new markets in California, Texas, and the Southwest. The consolidation also promised to save administrative costs, an estimated $100 million annual savings for 1996 alone.

Yet, in spite of the promised economy, the mergers failed to reduce costs, and employers grew increasingly anxious about the new upsurge in managed care premiums. By 1998, it was obvious that all was not well in the HMO market. Managed care premiums were on a double-digit rise, yet the old philosophy of denial and regulation remained firmly in place. The well-publicized merger mania of the previous years had failed to produce reduced premiums or improved benefits for enrollees. It was increasingly obvious that the HMO industry was concerned about the business, first and foremost. The cost-savings in the early 1990s had been a onetime event. The industry had failed to address the fatal flaws in the health care industry, and the hope of promise placed in the HMO concept had fallen short of expectations.

Not only were cracks beginning to appear in the financial infrastructure of the HMO industry itself, but a rising tide of resentment grew from the enrollees themselves. The fundamental principle underlying the HMO industry laid in regulating access of patients to physicians and providers. This was not a terribly sophisticated concept. Translating this into health care savings was seen as punitive and uncompromising. The name of the game was rationing.

Even before enrollment in a new HMO, prospective enrollees were required to complete in-depth health questionnaires about their personal well-being and that of their dependents. Preexisting conditions in the enrollee or any of their dependents invariably raised a red flag. Patients with chronic conditions such as diabetes or multiple sclerosis were either excluded from the group health plan or included only at unaffordable premiums. At best, coverage for the condition would only be offered after a considerable length of time, frequently up to several years, a practice known as directional ranking. Families of children with chronic conditions, such as cerebral palsy, were forced into remaining in the same employment indefinitely because of the overwhelming fear of losing their medical insurance. Since no preexisting condition would be covered by any new policy, families caring for sick individuals faced the real jeopardy of no insurance whatsoever. Prior to the HMO boom, many spouses fulfilled the role of homemaker, staying home with children. After the advent of the HMO, many were forced to enter the workforce, for the simple and overriding necessity of obtaining health insurance for their families.

Once enrolled in an HMO, employees soon faced the realities of a restricted choice of doctor and a bare-bones list of covered procedures. The list of participating providers was restricted to a panel of participating physicians, invariably those who were prepared to accept the cut-rate fee schedule. Referral to a specialist required preauthorization by the new primary care physician, who, more often than not, knew nothing about his or her new assignee. Having inherited a new influx of enrollees, primary care physicians became increasingly unavailable or were simply overwhelmed by the sheer number of HMO patients. Referral to a specialist was frequently regarded as a loss of faith in the new credo of "less is better." Incentives for nonreferral were commonplace, and for repeat offenders, removal from the HMO directory was the prescribed punishment. In practice, dealing with a primary care doctor was a pleasure compared to the bureaucratic nightmare of getting preauthorization from an HMO operative.

Preauthorization for a simple office visit routinely involved multiple phone calls and navigating an endless maze of punching numerals to reach the relevant department. Accumulated hours were then spent on hold, listening to tinny music until your call was eventually picked up. In the best of all scenarios, when a referral was obtained, this was for a limited number of visits, usually two or three, or for a defined period of time, usually two or three months. In the event that any diagnostic testing or procedure was required, this involved a repeat of the precertification process, obtaining ten- to fifteen-digit authorization numbers, and the faxing back and forth of a blizzard of paperwork. In the event the HMO denied the procedure, this involved a further campaign of phone calls until all but the most persistent providers fell by the wayside and resigned their patient to the realities of the new order of things.

To compound the agony, precertification of a surgical procedure had to be obtained not only from the physician but also for the hospital. This produced a simple doubling or tripling of effort. The cost in terms of man-hours and dollars was staggering. A study by the Cato Institute in 1999 estimated the administrative costs of HMOs at $33 billion per year. Some other institutes estimate much larger figures, up to $100 billion per year expended in bureaucracy, or 25 percent of the HMO sector's annual revenue.

If these hurdles and obstacles were negotiated successfully and the patient underwent the procedure, the process became yet more in-depth and intense. From the first day after surgery, the patient's progress was monitored by a utilization review nurse who reported to the HMO, the hospital, or both. Depending on the procedure, stickers appeared on the patient's chart on day two, three, or four, indicating that the health plan had preauthorized a number of hospital days for the patient's postoperative recovery. Any indications that the patient may have been making a satisfactory progress intensified activity from the utilization reviewer, and the number of colored stickers on the patient's chart increased proportionately. Failure to discharge the patient on the appointed day frequently led to a phone call from the health plan, demanding the patient be discharged, informing that coverage had been terminated on that day. Hospitalization beyond this period required a further campaign of phone calls, justification, and second-guessing by utilization review.

Rationing of health care by restricting patient access to providers was the bedrock principle of the HMO concept. Hand-in-hand with this principle, the HMO industry implemented additional and supporting strategies to limit health care costs further. The first of these was to slash reimbursement rates paid to providers, hospitals, and physicians in compensation for their services. Traditionally, insurance companies had used Medicare reimbursement rates as the yardstick for reimbursing physicians for both office visits and procedures performed. In the early 1990s, commercial carriers (i.e., non-Medicare or Medicaid) set this rate at some fraction above Medicare rates, usually 120 percent to 150 percent of what were regarded as rock-bottom Medicare figure. As the HMOs cut ever deeper into the number of participating physicians, the reimbursement rates for procedures sank ever more quickly toward the Medicare figure. By the end of the 1990s, this figure sank even further, below the Medicare rate, which was itself being reduced annually by Congress.

In 1993, Medicare reimbursement to consult a surgeon for a problem of intermediate complexity, the visit usually lasting between thirty and forty-five minutes, was $150. By 1998, this figure had dropped to $85. Commercial insurance in 1993 reimbursed an average of $200 for the same consultation. By 1998, the Aetna US Healthcare rate was $60, United Healthcare, $50, and Blue Cross/Blue Shield, $55. Medicare, widely regarded in the medical profession as a bare-bones payer, had achieved the status of pace setter, with the added attraction that Medicare usually paid its bills, unlike a great many of HMOs.

Reimbursement rates for surgical procedures followed the same pathway. In 1993, Medicare reimbursed physicians $900 for performing a colonoscopy on one of their enrollees. By 1999, this figure had been reduced to $300. In 1993, commercial indemnity plans reimbursed on average $1,500 per colonoscopy. By 1998, the burgeoning HMO industry reimbursed an average of $240 per procedure. The race to the bottom reached its climax in 1998, in the arena of cardiac surgery, a high-volume and high-cost subspecialty, and a favorite target for cuts. In 1998, Blue Choice Health Plan, a for-profit subsidiary of the Blue Cross/Blue Shield plan, reimbursed cardiac surgeons $1,000 for performing coronary artery bypass grafts on their enrollees. This two- to three-hour procedure involved opening the chest of their patients, stripping the leg veins to provide vascular grafts, and bypassing blocked coronary arteries to revascularize blood-starved heart muscle. The surgeon then carried the patient through an often stormy postoperative period and returned them back to health, all for the cost of a car engine tune-up. Office visits were also included in the discount price for a period of three months after the surgery.

The second pillar of faith to dissuade their enrollees from seeking medical health was the introduction of annual deductibles and the implementation of copayments for office visits and procedures. By dipping into the pockets of their own enrollees, the HMOs used this very effective financial deterrent as a mainstay against medical costs. As the HMO industry faced lagging profits in the mid-1990s and incurred increasingly heavy financial losses toward the end of the decade, copays and deductibles climbed relentlessly. The deductibles ranged from several hundred to several thousand dollars, depending on the type of coverage, and copays climbed closer and closer to the ever-shrinking costs of the office visit itself. The role of the HMO was rapidly becoming obsolete.

Early dissatisfaction with the denial tactics of HMOs led the health plans to introduce more lenient coverage for their enrollees, albeit at sharply increased premium rates. These included the preferred provider organization (PPO) and point-of-service plans (POS), a close relative to the traditional indemnity or fee-for-service plans. A spectrum of plans evolved, extending from the most restricted HMO plans, with little or no choice of provider, covering a very restricted range of procedures and providing the largest number of hurdles and impediments, such as mandatory referral by a primary care doctor, preauthorization to see a specialist, and precertification for any test or procedure. For a sharply higher premium, patients were allowed access to a larger number of providers offering a wider range of covered procedures. Referral by a primary care doctor was not always necessary, although preauthorization and precertification for procedures remained a mainstay. Annual deductibles for the POS option were hiked, and copays were pegged higher to maintain the disincentive.

The more lenient PPO and POS plans allowed their own enrollees to see out-of-network doctors, but this provision demanded higher premiums, plans reimbursed less for out-of-network doctors, and the blizzard of paperwork that this required dissuaded most from veering from the straight and narrow.

Chapter 8

BACKLASH

BY THE MID-1990S, THE PHILOSOPHY OF DENIAL AND dogma of bureaucracy led to a groundswell of revolt in the American public, who were accustomed to unlimited access and free choice of doctors. From 1994 until 1997, the HMO industry had managed to rein in costs, medical inflation was brought under control, and plan premiums remained relatively stable. Then they began to lose their grip. The cost savings introduced by rationing health care, restricting providers, and slashing fees proved to be a one-time event and not the systemic cure that had been promised. By 1997, the HMO industry was losing money. Growing demands from enrollees and increasing pressure from overburdened providers forced the HMOs to slacken their choking grip on health care delivery.

Horror stories surrounding HMOs denial of care or refusal to supply their promised services made more frequent headlines in the press. *Death by HMO, Don't Let Your HMO Kill You*, and similar titles became best sellers. In the late 1990s, HMOs became a byword for rationing, denial, and bureaucracy.

Having attracted 127 million Americans into the new face of managed care, the HMO industry was forced to account to almost half the nation for its shortcomings and pitfalls. Faced with increasing pressure to offer greater access to physicians and fewer restrictions on consumer choice, the HMOs were, in turn, forced to increase premiums to remain profitable. Freeing up access rules and relaxing denied services caused the industry to stop and contemplate its own philosophy. As Paul Ellwood correctly pointed out, "When the HMOs lose the ability to ration, the game is over."

By 1997, the HMO industry as a whole reported a loss of $490 million. This included $175 million loss by UnitedHealthcare, $60 million by Prudential Health Care, and $16 million by the nation's largest health insurance, Aetna HMO.

The financial crisis was not limited to the for-profit sector. Kaiser Permanente, the flagship of the nonprofit HMO industry, reported its first-ever financial losses of $266 million in 1997. The erosion was gradual but persistent: For the three years preceding the historic loss, profits had declined from $816 million to $550 million to $265 million. With 8.6 million enrollees in several states, Kaiser was forced to impose a premium hike of 20 percent. Having announced its historic losses, the grandfather of managed care announced an equally historic bonus for its CEO, David Lawrence. With a 1997 compensation package of $1.4 million, a 16 percent increase over the previous year, Kaiser's CEO, in a rare moment of introspection, generously agreed to forego any performance-related bonuses for the following year. Predicting premium hikes as high as 30 percent for 1999, Kaiser was forced to close down operations in several states. As the not-for-profit giant developed a severe case of severe dyspepsia, many recent acquisitions were jettisoned as part of a nationwide slimming-down operation.

The frenzy of mergers and acquisitions leading up to the 1997 slump became a thing of the past. The frenzy for HMO mergers, physician group buyouts, and hospital takeovers dropped 27 percent from its record high in 1997. With HMO fortunes taking turns for the worse, the relentless climb of the plan's stock price staggered and started a long trek downward. Faced with a growing gap between costs and premiums, the already beleaguered HMOs faced peril from a different quarter: the threat of class action lawsuits against HMOs by disgruntled or disabled enrollees, claiming denial of care under their HMOs.

The linchpin of this movement was an Illinois woman whose appendix ruptured during the three-day delay while awaiting an ultrasound at a facility owned by her HMO. The plaintiffs alleged that the HMO neglected their fiduciary responsibility to the patient by making her wait for the test at one of their own radiology facilities, whose rates were discounted by a contract with the HMO, rather than schedule the test at an outside facility, which would have cost the plan the standard rate. The delay culminated in a ruptured appendix, requiring emergency surgery and a prolonged recovery. Hitherto, HMOs had been shielded from such lawsuits by a provision under federal law known by its acronym, ERISA (Employer Retirement Security Act). The federal legislation, which preempted state law, prevented such lawsuits against HMOs from being held in state court, where rules of evidence were less stringent and jury awards were potentially multimillion blockbusters.

ERISA was originally designed to protect large multistate corporations from highly complex and seemingly random state laws related to their employee benefits packages—in this case, health care insurance provision. The legislation was designed to protect corporations from being "picked to death" by differing legislation from state to state and to allow protection under a blanket federal regulation. The denial of lawsuits under state law required plaintiffs to bring their cases to federal court, where rules of evidence were more stringent, thus making it more difficult for plaintiffs to prevail. Even if the HMO lost its case in federal court, financial awards were curtailed, compared to state court, making the whole venture unprofitable for a potential plaintiff. As the 1990s wore on, even the traditional legal firewall the HMOs had enjoyed seemed vulnerable: Plaintiffs lawyers found new ways to short-circuit the ERISA law, and disgruntled patients increasingly sued their health plans for failure to provide care, leaving the HMOs open to multimillion-dollar suits in state court.

The late 1990s saw the first casualties of the HMO industry filing for chapter 11 bankruptcy protection. In 1998, the San Diego–based FPA Medical Management was the first to go under, as chaos increasingly seized the health care industry. Pittsburgh-based Allegheny Health Foundation, one of the most aggressive not-for-profit health care systems, followed one month later. The winnowing of the HMO herd had started. Aetna, the Hartford, Connecticut, giant, experienced acute indigestion after a series of mergers starting in 1996 with US Healthcare. Faced with ballooning medical costs and difficulties integrating and assimilating its newly acquired plans, Aetna was punished by its shareholders, who dumped its stock, causing it to fall to levels not seen in eight years. Forced to sell off its profitable services and international business to a Dutch conglomerate, Aetna isolated its health care business in an attempt to stop the rot. Again, the only individual to emerge smiling was Aetna's chief executive, William H. Donaldson, who was promised a bonus of $2 million annually to manage the new health care subsidiary. The $2 million bonus was in addition to his $1 million annual base salary, one hundred thousand shares of stock, and options on a further five hundred thousand Aetna shares. Aside from his base salary and bonus, the stock options totaled an excess of $30 million dollars, the equivalent of the entire health budget of a small nation. Aetna shareholders were faring less well. While the stock price was around forty dollars per share in 1992, Aetna's shares peaked around $120 five years later in 1997. As the realities of the HMO industry became apparent to all on Wall Street, investors dumped Aetna stock, which fell to around fifty dollars by the year 2000.

The same story can be told of many of the leading lights in the HMO industry. Kentucky-based Humana shares, priced around six dollars in 1992, peaked at over thirty dollars in mid-1998. By the year 2000, the share price was continuing a linear dive to its former value of six dollars. UnitedHealthcare, which started at around fifty dollars a share in late 1994, peaked in early 1998 at over seventy dollars per share. By 2000, the stock price had fallen back to its level of six years previously.

Oxford Health plans provided the most stunning example of financial reversal. In late 1993, the HMOs share price was approximately fifteen dollars a share. After a series of highly publicized mergers and acquisitions, the stock soared to over eighty-five dollars per share in mid-1997. A fundamental and near-fatal failure to integrate the information technology of its recent acquisition led Oxford to underestimate its financial responsibilities drastically, and the HMO was engulfed in an information technology crisis of the first order. Almost overnight, Oxford's stock declined from seventy dollars to twenty dollars a share. Never recovering from the blow, its stock continued to erode over the next three years, to reach the fifteen-dollar value of seven years previously.

Traditionally, the early nonprofit HMOs had spent up to 95 percent of premiums on the delivery of medical care to its enrollees. The percentage, known cynically as the "medical-loss ratio," is calculated as the percentage of premiums spent on delivery of health care. The figure was used as a good-housekeeping seal of approval for plan enrollees. As the HMO industry turned to for-profit status, the medical-loss ratio was looked on in a completely different light. It was included in the annual corporate financial statement, and increasingly, investors looked critically at the figure to ensure that the premium dollar was not being squandered unnecessarily on the delivery of health care.

In the mid-1990s, as the stampede to Wall Street was in full flight, the medical-loss ratio quoted by the leading lights in the HMO industry sank to previously unheard of figures. Oxford Health plan led the pack by consistently maintaining the medical-loss ratio below 75 percent. In the fourth quarter of 1994, US Healthcare set a new industry record of a 68 percent ratio. By maintaining the "loss" well below par, the publicly traded companies were rewarded with an upsurge in stock evaluation and swelling market capitalization. Flush with cash in the mid-1990s, the health plans built lavish corporate office buildings as monuments to their newfound prestige and wealth. As the decade wore on, and as medical costs outstripped increases in premium, the medical-loss ratio became the victim of a simple mathematical equation. The much-applauded figures of 70 percent, 75 percent, and 80 percent soon disappeared from the annual report, and the ratios were forced increasingly to 85 percent and 90 percent.

These figures, which had not been seen for decades, were not a result of newfound generosity on the part of the publicly traded HMOs but were the inevitable result of the increasing financial pressures bearing on them. The financial pressures were passed on as premium hikes to their enrollees. In a study published by the Hay Group, a Philadelphia-based management consulting firm, health benefit costs had been held in check at 5–6 percent premium hikes up until 1998. According to the Hay Group, employers faced additional $544 out of pocket for an average fee-for-service plan, an increase of 4.2 percent. For a family PPO plan, the rate hike was $497. For a POS plan, the employer was forced to dig for a further $500, a 5 percent increase. HMO plans sustained the smallest increases at 3.1 percent annual hikes, or $446 for an average family premium. According to figures from William M. Mercer, a New York health care consultant, the average health care benefits, stood at $4,164 per employee in 1998. This represented a 6 percent hike over 1997. Large employers bore the brunt of the rate hikes, averaging health care costs to $4,567 per enrollee. Smaller employers faced smaller per capita costs, an average of $3,598 per employee. However, this represented a steeper increase over 1997, a 7.2 percent hike. By the year 2000, employers were faced with yet steeper rate increases, between 10–15 percent price hikes.

In the mid-1990s, at the peak of the HMO blitz, plan administrators looked to capitation as the wave of the future in order to rein in health costs. Under the model, an HMO made a set monthly payment for each enrollee, to provide health care services. Several versions of the capitation model were floated, the most comprehensive of which was global capitation. Under global capitation, hospitals and doctors assumed the risk for providing health care for the plans enrollees in return for a fixed per capita monthly payment. For providers, capitation had the attraction of providing a steady trickle, never a stream, of income and secured a large block of patients. The obvious downside to global capitation was that payments were deeply discounted and had usually been arrived at after a bidding war for the contract. The fear of being cut out of capitated contracts weighed more heavily on the minds of hospital administrators than did the reality of its economic consequences. The physicians reconciled their dilemma with the vain hope that access to a large block of patients would lead, in turn, to "knock-on" referrals to friends and family members. In short, many physicians accepted ludicrously low capitated contracts, simply to stay in the game.

Since physicians were being paid a monthly fee, irrespective of whether the patient was seen, the economic best-case scenario dictated that the patient should be seen as few times as possible or, preferably, not be seen at all. Faced with a professional responsibility to care for these patients, the doctor could not deny access. However, treatment options would be very carefully evaluated under the glaring realities of capitation.

Hard data does not exist illustrating procedures performed on capitated patients vs. fee-for-service models; however, faced with a nonlife- or limb-threatening situation—the choice between embarking on a conservative, noninvasive course of action in contrast to performing surgery or an invasive therapy—providers routinely chose the more conservative, lower-cost option. This almost inevitable consequence of capitation was not physician driven but was the logical conclusion of the HMO system in general, and the goal of the capitation model in particular. As experience with capitation grew, providers quickly realized the practically unavoidable financial downside of global-risk contracts. A single catastrophic case, such as an extremely premature neonate requiring months or weeks of ICU care, could soon turn a break-even risk contract deeply into the red. The hospitals were forced to absorb the deficits. The financial shortfall in capitation contracts for physician groups routinely amounted to millions of dollars, which was again absorbed by the group.

Capitation remained a more common form of payment for primary care physicians, who usually had a large patient base and low practice overhead and who infrequently performed procedures that consumed significant supplies or equipment. Specialists, such a surgeons or gastroenterologists, usually dealt with much smaller patient populations, much higher intervention rates, and much higher risks of resource-consuming complications. For these specialists, capitated contracts were a minefield to be avoided at all costs, if possible. Hospitals were uniquely vulnerable to the risks of global capitation since they lacked detailed demographic and financial data of the population for whom they had assumed the risk. In 1994, an article by *Modern Healthcare* reported 10.7 percent of hospital revenues came from capitated contracts. By 1997, this figure had fallen to 8.7 percent. Many of the losses sustained by hospitals in the capitated contracts were attributed to the lack of understanding of the actuarial risks involved. In a survey, *Modern Healthcare* also reported that 30 percent of hospital administrators have little understanding of their financial risks through capitated contracts.

The public, too, was quick to spot the obvious personal disadvantage from capitated health plans. As capitation rose, it was assumed that the capitation concept contained a self-righting system that in time would evolve and mature to the point that a financial equilibrium between insurers and providers would emerge. This "righting system," it was said, would provide a panacea for all, to cut losses and profits on both sides and provide harmony for all. "If a provider group met with wild success in one year and had massive profits, then its rate is going to go down the following year," explained National Health Information president David Schwartz. "Something is going to change in that contract so that the HMO is not allowing the provider to win as big." The converse is also held true: if providers lost the money during a contract year, then they negotiated higher rates for the following year to keep the system afloat. However, there was little harmony to be had from capitation. In California, where capitated plans gained an early foothold, medical groups who relied heavily on capitation could not make ends meet. The list of groups that became insolvent and filed for bankruptcy grew by the week. Capitation was becoming a dirty word.

Citing an "epidemic of capitation," the California Medical Association reported closure of over a hundred physician networks by 1999, their collapse directly attributable to capitation. The well-publicized failure of two medical networks, FPA Medical Management and Med Partners, focused national attention on California's problems. Both networks were placed into chapter 11 bankruptcy, and thousands of doctors were left with $100 million in unpaid capitation bills. Overall, 10 percent of California's capitated HMO networks became insolvent and closed. Physicians in failed groups were forced to seek new jobs and had to take out loans to stay afloat.

Price Waterhouse Cooper, called in by the California Medical Association to investigate the disaster, reported that the average capitation payment of $120 per member per month was almost $10 below the national average and well below the survival figure for financial viability. Quoting a common example in pediatrics, a California pediatrician's twenty-four-dollar monthly capitation fee did not cover the forty-seven dollars per month cost of immunizations, checkups, and childhood illnesses. America's doctors and hospitals looked anxiously at the California experience and, sustained by patient skepticism, moved increasingly away from capitation. Explained Mark Hyde, CEO of Lifeguard, a California HMO, "We are entering a period of de-capitation."

In the late 1990s, HMOs faced a triple threat to their future. The growing groundswell of discontent among the American public constituted their largest public relations challenge. Rising medical costs, greater medical-loss ratios, and plummeting stock prices threatened the financial viability of the industry. More sinister was the looming threat of class action lawsuits by patients alleging denial of care and erosion of the HMOs protection against lawsuits under the ERISA and RICO statutes.

ERISA, sponsored by longtime health care advocate Senator Jacob Javits, was originally hailed as the "greatest development in the life of the American worker since Social Security." This statute was intended to provide protection to large employers providing health and disability benefits to their employees. ERISA allowed self-insured employers protection against varying state regulations regarding health care plans. By an unintended and unanticipated accident of wording, ERISA provided blanket protection of the HMO industry against lawsuits from disgruntled enrollees. The plan, signed into law one year after the HMO act, was never intended to impact or regulate the HMO industry. However, the ERISA statute makes reference to "employee welfare benefit plans," which would be interpreted as employer-provided HMO health plans.

Protected for twenty-five years under the ERISA statute, the HMO plans cited the preemption clause stating ERISA "shall supersede any and all state laws insofar as made now or hereafter related to any employee benefit plan." This wording effectively provided the HMO industry blanket protection from state lawsuits and rendered state insurance laws meaningless. Under most state laws, an insurance company has an obligation to deal in "good faith" with its policyholders. Failure to do this held the company liable in state court for punitive damages. If that were proven, these punitive damages routinely exceeded the amount of the claim, which caused insurance companies to toe the line in processing and paying claims. Since ERISA preempted these "bad faith laws," the HMOs no longer had to fear the prospect of punitive damages in state court. This removed any requirement for any insurance company to treat the claimant fairly and, instead, relied on the goodwill and generosity of the company.

The odds were further stacked in favor of the HMO industry by the rules of evidence under ERISA, which placed tremendous burdens on any potential plaintiff to prove his case. Furthermore, ERISA provided no recourse for a successful plaintiff to claim any award for attorney fees for his case. Understandably, ERISA attorneys were few and far between. If the claimant was successful in winning his case and the disputed benefits were granted (minus punitive damages), then the plaintiff would be required to pay the attorney from his disputed benefit package, leaving him with little or nothing. Hence, the ERISA statute was seen by the HMO industry as one of its most valuable assets, sustaining its very existence.

However, the late 1990s saw a handful of pivotal cases appearing in state court and even one that reached the US Supreme Court. As mentioned earlier, Cynthia Herdrich, of Bloomington, Illinois, sued her health plan for failing to diagnose her appendicitis timely. An ultrasound exam was ordered by her physician; however, the test was delayed for three days to enable for it to be performed at a local facility owned by the HMO. Having already won a $35,000 medical malpractice lawsuit, Ms. Hedrick took her case to the US Supreme Court. The plaintiff challenged the HMOs exemption under ERISA, claiming that the practice of rewarding physicians to limit care violated the plans fiduciary duty to the patient. Arguments were heard in February of 2000, and the justices handed down the unanimous decision four months later, in June of 2000, ruling for the HMO. Justice David Souter wrote, "Provision of profit is what makes the HMO a proprietary organization, and this remedy in effect will be nothing less than the elimination of the for-profit HMO." Predictably, the HMO industry praised the ruling but privately conceded the battle was far from over. The state courts were increasingly asserting their willingness to look closer at the ERISA exemption and hold HMOs liable for the wellbeing of their enrollees.

One month before this US Supreme Court ruling, the Illinois Supreme Court ruled that HMOs could be held liable on a theory of "institutional negligence." The case involved Sheila Jones, who sued Chicago HMO. Jones called her physician when her three-month-old daughter became agitated and developed a fever. Not able to speak with the doctor, his assistant suggested giving the baby castor oil, since she was also constipated. The next day the patient took her baby to the emergency room where she was diagnosed with bacterial meningitis. The baby suffered permanent brain damage and required round-the-clock care. The Illinois Supreme Court agreed with Jones that the HMO had placed too great a burden on her physician by assigning him an excessive amount of patients. Responsible for over six thousand patients, the doctor was overburdened and failed to render the necessary care. State courts continued to find theories under which HMO plans can be held liable, and the Jones case was the opening salvo in a deluge of similar cases. The legal experts agreed that although the HMOs won a logistic battle in the US Supreme Court, they were losing the strategic campaign in the state courts and faced the prospects of losing the war. The prospect of a deluge of multimillion-dollar lawsuits certainly rested heavily on the HMO industry, and equally heavily on their investors, who walked away from the industry in increasing numbers.

The final source of legal jeopardy against the HMOs arose in the form of veteran class action lawyer, Richard Scruggs. Emerging victoriously from a class action lawsuit against the asbestos industry, and as one of the chief architects of a $246 billion state action against the tobacco industry, Richard Scruggs turned his attention to the HMOs. Assisted by David Boies, veteran of the Microsoft antitrust case, the duo filed a lawsuit against the HMO industry on behalf of 32 million enrollees. Alleging that HMOs reward their reviewers to reject claims and claiming that the internal appeals process is designed to exhaust patients "until they go away," Scruggs led a coalition of attorneys in an action filed against Humana,

Cigna Healthcare, Foundation Health Systems, Pacificare, and Prudential Health Care. "We are acting today to fix the broken promises that the HMO industry has made to the people who entrust their very lives to these companies," Scruggs explained.

Flush with cash from previous victories, these attorney cartels were able to finance lengthy and complicated litigation on a scale never before possible. The legal threat of protracted litigation and the possibility of an adverse ruling for the HMO would, at best, drive up medical costs and, at worse, may prove to be the beginning of the end for the industry. So with eroding protection under the ERISA statute, attorneys also turned to the antiracketeering laws as a new way to assail the industry. In a lawsuit filed against Humana, 84,000 plan enrollees sued under the Racketeer Influenced and Corrupt Organizations (RICO) Act, alleging that Humana negotiated secretly with hospitals to obtain discounts on hospital bills accrued by their enrollees. Having obtained the discount for the plan, Humana then failed to pass on the discount to their enrollees, who were liable for 20 percent of the bill. Similar allegations were leveled against Blue Cross and Blue Shield, many of which had already been settled.

By the late 1990s, the mass migration of patients from indemnity plans to HMOs had slowed to a trickle, and by the midpoint of 1999, HMOs posted their lowest recorded enrollment in ten years, a 2.6 percent increase over the previous year. More troubling, during the last six months of 1999, total enrollment actually dropped for the first time in the HMO history, by 0.6 percent. After peaking at 81.5 million members at the end of 1998, HMOs lost more than a half-million enrollees during the first six months of 1999. Faced with widespread disenchantment, increasing premiums, a hostile press, and a skeptical judiciary, the HMO had passed well beyond the growth phase as it struggled to define its goals for health care and its role in society.

Reviewing the evolution of the HMO, Paul Ellwood, (the father of the HMO), expressed mixed emotions in an interview with the *Journal of the American Medical Association* in December of 1998. "For those of us who devoted our lives to reshape the health industry, and where our motives were typical for many physicians, trying to make the health system better for patients, the thing has been a profound disappointment."

Chapter 9

OBAMACARE

AFTER THE WORLD TRADE CENTER DISASTER IN 2001, AND with two unpopular wars in Afghanistan and Iraq, health care reform took a backseat. In the background, an emergent crisis was evolving in the form of the impending US housing market collapse. Between 1998 and 2006, the typical American home increased in value by 124 percent. A housing bubble was emerging, and many homeowners refinanced their homes with adjustable rate mortgages based on their increased value of their property, or they took out second mortgages for consumer spending.

The surge in property values created "a giant pool of money," amounting to approximately $70 trillion in potential worldwide property investments. This was too much of a temptation for Wall Street to ignore. This investment was regarded as a safe risk and investment banks on Wall Street answered this demand with mortgage-backed securities, such as real estate investment trusts, and the collateralized debt obligation. These investment instruments were given triple-A credit ratings by rating agencies, such as Moody's.

From 2000 to 2005, Americans had extracted $5 trillion from their real estate equity and went on a spending binge. Wall Street expanded the collateralized debt obligation, based on the ballooning price of the American property market. Banks and financial institutions collected mortgage loans, placed them into a single pool, sliced and diced them, and sold these off to eager investors. The more reliable investment-grade instruments received lower rates of return, and the riskier, lower-credit instruments carried a higher rate, given their additional risk.

At the same time, the need for "affordable housing" was being promoted, primarily by Barney Frank, chairman of the House Financial Services Committee. The government agency financing the subprime properties was the Federal National Mortgage Association, otherwise known as Fannie Mae, established in 1938 by the Roosevelt administration in its New Deal legislation. Fannie Mae was a government agency established to inject liquidity into the economy and enable local banks to finance additional home mortgages in an attempt to raise levels of home ownership, especially affordable housing. The injection of federal funds into the housing sector added additional liquidity and enabled local banks to issue additional mortgages, which, in turn, were bought up by Fannie Mae. In 1992, the Community Reinvestment Act expanded the need for additional affordable housing. Fannie Mae and its younger sibling financier, Freddie Mac, were required by law to increase the quota of risky investments from 30% in 1992 to almost 60% in 2008, a doubling of high-risk mortgages. These loans were made to individuals below the medium income, with fewer or no tangible assets, and eventually without the ability to fund their mortgages. This push to increase home ownership was a bilateral and bipartisan process. The proportion of subprime loans increased to 50 percent under Clinton and 55 percent under George W. Bush in 2007. Home ownership, which was at 64 percent in 1982, increased to almost 68 percent In 2007, at the peak of the real estate bonanza.

Much of this was funded by Freddie Mae and Freddie Mac. At the peak of the bonanza, Freddie Mae and Freddie Mac owned approximately 70 percent of all US mortgages, and they were leveraged by a ratio of seventy-five to one, (i.e., for every dollar in the government coffers, seventy-five dollars was at risk). By 2007, 27 million mortgages, approximately half of all the mortgages in the United States, were subprime. Over 70 percent of these (19.2 million) were on the books of the government. The number of defaults on the mortgages increased steadily from mid-2006 to the pinnacle at 2008. As the holders of the subprime mortgages defaulted in increasing numbers, housing prices declined 20 percent during this period. Homeowners who had financed with adjustable rate mortgages were unable to refinance because of increasing interest rates, and the value of their properties imploded. In 2007, 1.3 million properties were placed in foreclosure, an 80 percent increase over the year before. In 2008, the number had increased to 2.3 million, and by August 2008, 9.2 percent of all mortgages were either delinquent or in foreclosure. A year later, this was 14.4 percent.

Since Freddie Mae and Freddie Mac were the principal owners of these defunct mortgages, trillions of dollars could potentially be lost by investors such as retirement funds, the Chinese government, and famously, Icelandic municipalities. At the peak of the crisis in 2008, Fannie Mae and Freddie Mac owned about $6 trillion of defunct mortgages. If the government entities became insolvent, the home mortgage industry would implode, mortgages would be impossible to find, and a financial crisis would ensue. The US Treasury stepped in to underpin Freddie Mae and Freddie Mac, and the national debt ceiling was increased by $800 billion to a total of $10.7 trillion in order to underpin the economy and prevent the collapse of the entire capitalist system.

A further complication in the housing crisis came in the form of the credit default swap, the financial instrument created by Blythe Masters of J.P. Morgan in London in 1994. The credit default is a guarantee issued by the seller against a loan default. If a loan is in default, of which 20 million were in 2008, the seller of the credit default swap makes good on the face value of the mortgage to the buyer. The notional value of these credit default swaps at the peak of the crisis in 2008 amounted to $62.2 trillion, or five times the GDP of the United States. These were referred to as a "nuclear financial weapon" by Warren Buffet. The US housing crisis by 2008 was at its peak, and the collapse of the entire financial system seemed imminent.

One of the first financial victims in the US market was Lehman Brothers, who, since 2003, had bought up several subprime lenders, such as BNC Mortgage. Lehman Brothers had acquired a disproportionate number of subprime loans and, therefore, were first in line over the cliff. The firm had bought $146 billion of mortgages in 2006 and reaped healthy profits. The stock reached eighty-six dollars in February 2007. As the housing market started to implode, Lehman Brothers also imploded. In March 2007, the stock price plummeted, and the company, contrary to the public statement of the chief financial officer, was insolvent. In March 2008, Lehman declared bankruptcy and lost $46 billion of its market value. The US Treasury did not intervene.

AIG, the major seller of credit defaults, was next in line. Faced with trillions of dollars of payments from delinquent mortgages and foreclosures, AIG's stock dropped 60 percent at the opening of the New York Stock Exchange on September 16, 2008. Fearing a complete collapse of the US economy, the Treasury stepped in that evening and created an $85 billion fund for a 79.9 percent equity in AIG, propping up the company. By May of the following year, government support would amount to $180 billion. The crisis came to a head in a dramatic meeting on September 18, 2008, when the treasury secretary, Hank Paulson, and then-chairman of the Federal Reserve, Ben Bernanke, met with administration leaders to announce a $700 billion TARP bailout fund. Faced with resistance, Bernanke's response was blunt: "If we do not do this, we may not have an economy on Monday."

The cost of the whole housing sector implosion has been calculated as a $5.2 trillion loss. Others estimate the cost of the crisis at well over $10 trillion. By comparison, the cost of the Vietnam War was approximately $800 million, and the Iraq war was $1.5 trillion.

Over eleven million Americans were out of work, and unemployment shot up to 10.1 percent, but real unemployment was estimated at more than 15 percent. As many as 9.3 million Americans lost their health insurance, and 11 million homeowners (one in four) had either lost their homes or were "underwater" with their home values.

The resulting credit crisis rolled over into the auto industry. In November 2008, two months after the federal meeting, General Motors, Chrysler, and Ford approached the government for a $50 billion loan to avoid bankruptcy. General Motors became yet another ward of the federal government. Faced with the financial disaster, the collapse of credit, and the implosion of the housing market, the Republicans were faced with an inevitable trouncing. Going into the 2008 elections, the Senate consisted of forty-nine Democrats, forty-nine Republicans, and two independents. After the dust had settled from the election, the Republicans lost eight seats to the Democrats, the largest political landslide for the Democrats since 1986. The Republicans were completely shut out of New England, the first time since the 1850s. The new Senate consisted of fifty-eight Democrats and forty-one Republicans, which, with the defection of Arlen Spector and the recount win of Al Franken in Minnesota, gave the Democrats a filibuster-proof majority of sixty to forty. The Democrats, anticipating a filibuster of any major health care reform, required sixty seats in order to close debate and bring the proceedings to a vote. Obtaining those sixty seats would turn out to be a knife-edge endeavor.

In his State of the Union Address in February of 2009, the new president, Barack Obama, announced his plans for health care reform. In the Senate, the Finance Committee held a series of closed-door meetings to discuss health care reform. The minimum requirement for the Obama administration was universal health care. The notion of a single payer (i.e., the federal government, the equivalent of Britain's National Health Service) was considered dead on arrival. The US Congress, compared to Britain's Parliament, is composed of a bell curve much to the right of Britain. Even the US Senate's most liberal members would hardly recognize Britain's Labor and Socialist members.

The central premise of the new bill, universal coverage with guaranteed issue, would require an individual mandate (i.e., the requirement of every American to purchase health care insurance). This had, in fact, been proposed by the Heritage Foundation, a conservative think tank, many years previously. They also had the support of many Republicans, although that support would rapidly be withdrawn. As the *New York Times* commentated, in the face of concrete Republican opposition to an individual mandate, "It can be difficult to remember now given the ferocity with which many Republicans assail it as an attack on freedom, but the provision in President Obama's health care law requiring all American's to buy health insurance has its roots in conservative thinking."

All spending bills in Congress are required to originate in the House of Representatives, and so the Senate took up House Bill 3590, a revenue bill requiring housing tax breaks for service members. This was used as a vehicle for the Affordable Care Act, and it would be ultimately tarnished as a tax issue. Throughout the summer of 2009, the Senate Finance Committee negotiated the elements of health care reform, confident of their sixty-vote filibuster-proof majority. On August 25, disaster struck with the death of Ted Kennedy, a longtime health care reform veteran. The Democrats were now back to fifty-nine votes. During the scramble for the sixtieth vote, the issue of the public option was heatedly contested. The public option was a federally sponsored health plan that would compete with private health insurance and other vehicles. Finally, in order to obtain the sixtieth vote, the public option was dropped and Nebraska's Ben Nelson, the conservative Democrat, provided the final vote for a filibuster-proof majority. The final vote of the Senate was fifty-eight Democrats and two independents voting yes and all Republicans voting no. On December 24, Christmas Eve, 2009, the final vote was held with endorsement by the AMA and

AARP. In January 2010, before the House could complete its negotiations and the bill could be referred back to the Senate for its final vote, the election of Scott Brown, a Republican, to fill Ted Kennedy's seat, was a shock to the system. Finally, the House acquiesced to the Senate provisions, and the final bill, the Affordable Care Act, was signed on March 30, 2010.

The final bill guaranteed universal coverage, with guaranteed issue, without individual ratings, (i.e., preexisting conditions) were excluded and an individual mandate for all Americans except illegal immigrants. Other elements include a state-sponsored health care exchange and private health care provisions, which were subject to minimum requirements.

Five years after passage of the Affordable Care Act, most of the state exchanges are either insolvent or closed down. Not one of the remaining co-operatives are making a profit and insurance premiums of those remaining plans are set to increase by double-digit percentages.

The California exchange in 2014 faced an $80 million deficit after 300,000 people less than expected enrolled. In 2015 New York's exchange, the largest co-operative created under the Affordable Care Act, was closed by state and federal insurance regulators as it plunged into insolvency. Minnesota's exchange required a $34 million infusion from federal tax funds, and Rhode Island, Vermont, and most other state exchanges face similar fates. From 2014 to 2016, co-ops closed their doors at a rapid rate, as losses escalated. By the end of 2016, only seven of the original twenty-three exchanges will remain open, leaving an estimated 800,000 Americans scrambling to find alternative insurance, and the American taxpayer on the hook for $2.4 billion in start-up "loans". However, amongst all the chaos a familiar theme remained. According to *The Daily Caller,* eighteen of the twenty-three co-ops were paying their top executives handsomely for their efforts, up to $500,000 dollars a year.

Meanwhile, among the private health insurers, a flurry of mergers and acquisitions took place. The private insurers seemingly clinging to each other for safety and support as they are sucked down the financial drain. Anthem and Cigna entered a blockbuster merger. Aetna purchased Humana for $37 billion, Anthem purchased Cigna for $48 billion, and the prospect of just three or four major health care insurance companies is now a reality. As only a handful of major private health insurers remain standing, six years after the passage of the Affordable Care Act, they face a similar fate to Lehman Brothers, AIG, General Motors, and Chrysler, when the federal government stepped in to prop them up. When this day dawns the much-feared reality of a single payer national health care system (i.e., the US taxpayer) becomes a reality.

Chapter 10

COST OF LIVING

BY THE 1970'S, THE BRITISH NATIONAL HEALTH SERVICE was the second largest employer in the world, employing over one million workers, second only to the Red Army in the USSR. Funding of this behemoth was from direct taxation distributed from the Treasury to the Department of Health and to the district health regions. Funding was by "trickle down" financing, expenditure was fixed, but there was little real accountability. R. J. Maxwell, chief executive of the King's Fund, the UK health care think tank, described NHS funding as "the limestone cliff." "The flow of expenditure is like the flow of water through a limestone cliff. You can measure the flow at the top in the central allocation of funds by Her Majesty's Treasury, and you can perceive the details of thousands of individual clinical decisions at the bottom. There is a connection between the two (as it were within the rock face) that is so elusive," he explained. Margaret Thatcher in her book *The Downing Street Years* had another geological analogy for the NHS. "The NHS was a bottomless pit," she quipped bluntly.

By Margaret Thatcher's election in May of 1979, after decades of industrial disputes, union strikes, work-to-rules, high inflation, soaring unemployment, and an IMF bailout, the National Health Service was in bad shape.

Recognizing that the National Health Service required urgent modernization and major structural reforms, she invited Professor Alain Enthoven, a health economist from Stanford University, to propose reform. In a six-month sabbatical to the United Kingdom, Enthoven concluded that "the NHS is, like New York traffic, gridlocked," and it needed to be freed up.

This caused significant disquiet in the medical community and the public at large. *The Lancet* described Enthoven's intervention as "Margaret Thatcher's reliance on the health policy advice of the Vietnam-era Pentagon war planner adds to our disquiet."

Enthoven recognized the need for competition and proposed "the internal market" to introduce competition in the NHS. The need for basic market principles was recognized and major reform of the NHS was undertaken. The distribution of funds was placed on committees of general practitioners, who acted as gatekeepers, originally referred to as "trusts," and more recently, "clinical commission groups." The GP allocated funds to the newly created health care trusts, which would compete with each other according to their performance. In 1998, the National Health Service published its first report in fifty years as to how its funds were spent. "Reference costs" were published for each of the health care trusts, and for the first time, the report documented the number of each type of medical case performed and the nominal cost of each of these cases.

This was the first time the NHS was accountable for its expenditures. This also provided the opportunity for outside review of the NHS performance.

Similar data has long been available in the United States, although it is fragmented, often incomplete, and outdated. From its creation, the Center for Medicare and Medicaid Services (CMS) has published data on its expenditures. Similarly, other economic and survival data is available from the government and private sources: Department of Health and Human Services (HHS), the National Center for Health Statistics, the US Census Bureau, the National Institute of Health (NIH), the Centers for Disease Control (CDC), the American Cancer Society (ACS), the National Center for Biotechnology Information (NCBI), the American Medical Association (AMA), the American Hospital Association (AHA), and the Kaiser Foundation.

In the United Kingdom, the sources include the National Health Service (NHS), NHS Reference Costs, Office for National Statistics (ONS), Department of Health (DoH), World Health Organization (WHO), and private or semiprivate entities such as UK Cancer Research, the British Medical Association (BMA), the British Medical Journal (BMJ), and the Nuffield Foundation. Much data is unavailable. Health insurance companies do not publish proprietary data, and direct comparison between US and UK health care expenditures is incomplete at best. Nonetheless, broad trends are discernable, and it is possible to make very broad comparisons of major health issues between the United Kingdom and the United States.

In the United Kingdom, over 90 percent of health care spending is consumed by National Health Services spending, a single-payer, single-provider system. In the United States, private health care insurance accounts for 64 percent of spending, Medicaid 16 percent, and Medicare 15 percent. Prior to the Affordable Care Act, 15 percent of the population, or 48 million, were uninsured. After the first few years of the act, this dropped to 12 percent and 40 million, respectively. Given the chasm in spending between the United Kingdom and the United States, and in light of recently published NHS reference costs, it is possible to identify the pros and cons of a mature socialist system versus a quasi-free market system as in the United States.

In 1948, shortly after the inception of the NHS, per capita health care costs in Britain were around £800 ($1,200) in inflation-adjusted dollars and increased on average at the glacial pace of 2 percent per annum. In contrast in the United States, health care costs increased on average 8 percent per annum, a rate four times that of Britain, and, more importantly, four times the average inflation rate in the United States over the last fifty years. In 2015, health care costs in the United Kingdom remained around 9 percent of GDP, or about $3,000 per capita. In the same year, US health care costs reached almost 17 percent of GDP, about $9,000 per capita. Doubtless, these numbers would have been much higher in the United States had not the Great Recession intervened. Great recessions tend to sink all boats equally.

Total government spending in the United States averages 33 percent of GDP, absent wars or major recessions, compared to 45 percent in Britain, reflecting much higher costs of the "social safety net" in Britain: healthcare, pensions, education, child benefits, long-term care, and unemployment/disability.

Health care inflation had an impact on government-run programs as well as the private sector. In 1996, the trustees of the Medicare Trust Fund reported that Medicare was projected to enter insolvency by 2001, in a shortfall of $53 billion, a result of the aging population and the rampant health care inflation in the 1990s. The Great Recession of 2007/8 resulted in one significant benefit: insolvency of the Medicare Trust Fund was pushed back to 2030. Nonetheless, an aging population poses a bleak future for Medicare's funding at current levels. In 1995, there were 3.9 workers per beneficiary; in 2030, it is estimated there will be 2.2 workers per beneficiary. Short-term redress would require a 39 percent cut in services or a 63 percent increase in income to the fund.

The frugal funding of the NHS is reflected in the available medical manpower to treat the British public. In 2000, NHS employed 68,460 salaried physicians, including hospital doctors and GPs. During the same time period, there was a total of 650,000 physicians in the United States, a per capita rate double that in the United Kingdom. The proportion of specialists and subspecialists in the United States outstrips that in the United Kingdom. In the United States, of the 650,000 physicians, 450,000 are specialists or subspecialists, and 200,000 primary care, a situation where specialists outnumber primary care by a ratio of two to one, the opposite scenario to Britain. Doubtless, this schism in the ratio of specialists to primary care/GPs is responsible, in part, to the much greater costs of health care in the United States. However, as we will see, there is a definite price to pay in terms of higher mortality rates in Britain.

The training level of physicians in the United States versus the United Kingdom is also starkly different. At any time in the

United States, there are 97,000 trainee physicians (residents or fellows) compared to 650,000 fully fledged and licensed practitioners. The ratio is, therefore, one trainee to seven trained doctors. In the United Kingdom, this same ratio in Britain is one to one, reflecting much longer "apprenticeships" for junior doctors in the United Kingdom in order to maintain the number of medical "boots on the ground" to fill the NHS. US primary care or specialty training is typically three to five years, depending on the nature of the practice. Training is, therefore, structured and finite. In the United Kingdom, medical specialty training is a hierarchy, with ever-increasing levels of rank or seniority and lacking finite or defined duration of training programs. As frustrating and even unfair as this is for the "junior" doctors in the United Kingdom, it keeps the ranks of the NHS physicians filled to capacity to meet manpower needs.

The number of hospitals and per capita hospital beds reflects the same differential in funding between systems. In British hospitals, the NHS boasts 558 acute hospitals and a total of 108,000 acute beds, or 160 beds per 100,000 population. In the United States, there are 5,057 hospitals (3,000 not-for-profit; 797 investor-owned, for-profit; and 1,260 state and local government). The total of 853,287 acute beds translates to 390 beds per 100,000 population, over twice that available in the United Kingdom. The average US hospital is much smaller (168 beds) compared to the larger NHS infirmaries (average 354 beds). US hospitals purchase much more capital equipment to compete in the marketplace (e.g., MRIs, CTs, Lithotripsy, PET scanners). Hospital costs, therefore, soar in the United States compared to the United Kingdom.

Not surprisingly, the number of hospital admissions in the United States versus the United Kingdom were disproportionately high: 30,545 versus. 9,962 per 100,000 population, or a three-to-one ratio in favor of the United States. Total surgeries performed in the United States versus the United Kingdom were 34,854 versus 4,964 per 100,000, or a seven-to-one ratio, higher in the United States. Per capita, seven times as many surgeries are performed in the United States compared to the United Kingdom. Emergency room admissions are also double the rate in the United States, reflecting the overall greater access to emergency and non-emergency health care.

Not every disease can be prevented, in spite of the most advanced technology, and some diseases are too rare to allow meaningful analysis of medical intervention or costs incurred. For example, lymphoma is a very uncommon malignancy of the lymphatic system, which is evenly distributed in the United States and the United Kingdom. There are no screening programs for lymphoma, and once it is identified, there are no surgical interventions other than chemotherapy to treat it. In addition, mortality is high, so outcomes are very difficult to compare between populations. Conversely, lung cancer is very common in both the United States and the United Kingdom; in fact, it is the most common malignancy on both sides of the Atlantic. Although the incidence is high, making it a potentially useful yardstick for measuring outcomes, there is no useful population screening procedure and no effective therapy. Mortality is so high (90 percent at five years) that, irrespective of whatever resources may be available and treatments delivered, no difference will be found between populations.

To compare health care between two populations, the index diseases must be common, susceptible to population screening, and amenable to intervention with an aim to cure, and the mortality must be sufficiently low to compare outcomes between nations. If the incidence of a disease is not sufficiently large, the number of individuals afflicted will not be large enough to compare national outcomes.

If the disease cannot be detected by mass population screening, if early detection is not possible, an intervention for a possible cure is impossible. If the disease is not amenable to surgical or other treatments, then the best medical system in the world would not produce any positive outcome. If the death rate from the disease is too high, then again the best health system in the world will fail to produce a discernible difference.

For purposes of comparison, three diseases were examined. The first disease was breast cancer, which can be detected at an early stage by population screening. Early intervention can lead to a potential cure or prolongation of life. Having detected breast cancer, it can be treated aggressively with lumpectomy, radiation, or mastectomy, with good results. Mortality for breast cancer over a prolonged ten-year period is approximately 50 percent, so comparisons can be made.

The second disease studied was colorectal cancer. This is the third most common carcinoma after breast cancer, and it can be detected at an early stage and either cured in the polyp stage by endoscopic polypectomy or resected in the early stages of carcinoma, with ten-year survivals of approximately 60 percent.

The third disease, ischemic heart disease, the most common cause of death both in the United States and the United Kingdom, is not commonly amenable to mass population screening, but when identified can be effectively treated by aggressive intervention such as angioplasty and cardiac stents or commonly, bypass graft. If treated early and effectively, mortality can be reduced dramatically and therefore, be used as a yardstick for population comparisons.

Looking first at breast cancer, data from the CDC cites the number of mammograms performed in the United States in 2000 as over 7,000 per 100,000 population, compared to approximately 4,000 per 100,000 population in the United Kingdom. Resulting biopsies in the United States was 230 per 100,000, compared to 39 in the United Kingdom. Population deaths in the United States from breast cancer were approximately forty thousand, compared to fourteen thousand in the United Kingdom. Given the fivefold difference in population in the United States versus the United Kingdom, this translated to 12 deaths per 100,000 in the United States, compared to 22 per 100,000 in the United Kingdom, almost twice the rate. This confirms that a more aggressive screening program in the United States for breast cancer translates to a lower death rate and higher longevity. According to a 2011 OECD study, five-year survival for breast cancer in the United States was 89.3 percent, compared to 81.3 percent in Britain.

Next, colon cancer: Colonoscopy screening for colon cancer reflects a similar schism. Approximately 2.5 million colonoscopies were performed in the United States, compared to 135,000 in the United Kingdom. This translates to a five-to-one differential in the colonoscopy rate in favor of the United States.

Population deaths from colorectal cancer in the United States were just over fifty thousand compared to seventeen thousand in the United Kingdom. This translates to 14 per 100,000 people dying of colorectal cancer in the United States, compared to 26 per 100,000 in the United Kingdom, almost twice the rate. Due to a lack of screening colonoscopy, the death rate from colorectal cancer is therefore almost double the rate in the United Kingdom. According to the same 2011 OECD study, five-year survival for colon cancer in the United States was 64.5 percent, compared to 53.3 percent in Britain.

Finally, treatment of ischemic heart disease is strikingly different in the United States and the United Kingdom. Diagnosis of ischemic heart disease, once symptoms begin, is commonly an angiogram, followed either by angioplasty to dilate the narrowing in the coronary artery or placement of a cardiac stent. If this fails, the patient requires a coronary artery bypass graft (CABG) by opening the chest and bypassing one or more multiple cardiac vessels to revascularize the heart. In the United States, 2.5 million cardiac angiograms and angioplasties were performed, compared with approximately fifty thousand in the United Kingdom This translates to a ten or twenty times difference in the intervention in cardiac angiography in the United States versus the United Kingdom.

If surgical revascularization of the heart is required, these numbers are repeated, with approximately six hundred thousand CABG grafts performed in the United States versus twenty thousand in the United Kingdom. This reflects six-to-one differential in favor the United States.

When death from ischemic heart disease is examined, there is a clear benefit in the US population versus the United

Kingdom. A recent international comparison of thirty-day mortality after a heart attack in OECD states put the death rate in the United States as 6.1 percent, compared to 9.4 percent in the United Kingdom, a 50 percent hike in death rates in the United Kingdom. The differential in stroke deaths (cerebrovascular accidents) was even more pronounced. Thirty-day death rates from stroke in the United Kingdom were 14.8 percent, compared to 4.4 percent in the United States, or over a threefold differential.

Cost comparisons are even more difficult than the basic incidence of procedures performed. When data from the CDC and CMS is compared with the National Health Service reference cost, the average cost of procedures in the US averages about 1.5 times more than the same or similar procedures in the United Kingdom. Given the very strict budgetary constraints of the NHS and the obvious differences in funding between the United States and the United Kingdom, the cost differential is hardly surprising.

The bottom line with breast cancer and colon cancer is that early, aggressive screening produces lower mortality and longer life expectancy, albeit at greater financial cost. For cardiac disease, aggressive intervention using cardiac angiograms, angioplasty, and stents, coronary artery disease results in lower cardiac mortality and increased life expectancy.

These outcomes have even been reported by British researchers, leading to an uproar in the British press. For the past ten years, Professor Brian Jarman, professor of statistics from Imperial College London, studied the performance of the NHS and compared this to several OECD countries. He found poorer cancer survival; longer waiting lists; lower rates of diagnostic procedures, such as angiography, angioplasty, CABG graft, and MRI; along with fewer physicians and hospital beds, per capita population.

Professor Jarman also developed an index to measure hospital mortality rates between hospitals and even between countries: the Hospital Standard Mortality Ratio (HSMR).

HSMRs measure hospital mortality rates, taking into account patients' ages and severity of illnesses, and are used to compare rates between hospitals. If death rates are within the expected range, the hospital scores an HSMR of 100. If mortality is lower than expected, they score under 100, and if mortalities were higher than expected, they score over 100.

HSMRs in the NHS were 58 percent higher than the best country, the United States. In 2012, a patient in the average NHS hospital was 45 percent more likely to die in the hospital than if they had been admitted to a US hospital.

Patients over sixty-five were five times more likely to die of pneumonia in an NHS hospital and twice as likely to die from septicemia when compared to a US hospital. The majority of US hospitals scored under 100 (i.e., lower mortalities), whereas the majority of NHS hospitals scored between 100–150, i.e. higher mortalities. The average HSMR for NHS hospitals was 122.4, whereas the average HSMR for US hospitals was 77.4. NHS hospitals scored the worst of all seven OECD countries studied.

Chapter 11

LEHMAN BROTHERS 2.0

GIVEN THE FREQUENT AND HEATED DEBATES ABOUT health care provision in both the United States and the United Kingdom, the obvious question is this: what is the right solution? The short answer is that there is no single solution for the United Kingdom and certainly not in the United States. In the United Kingdom, the National Health Service is not only a single-payer system (the government) but also a single-provider system (the government). All physicians (myself included, twenty-five years ago) are employed by the National Health Service and, therefore, are employed by the government. For the British patient, choice of doctor is limited, the waiting list is long, procedures performed are severely restricted, and eligibility for care is limited. As Alan Milburn, Labour health minster, famously stated, "The NHS is woven into the fabric of British society." For a litany of reasons, such a system would never prevail in the United States.

By contrast, in the United States, during the 2009 health care debate, a single-payer system was narrowly defeated in the US Congress. Already passed by the House, the Senate concluded a single-payer option could not get a fifty-one-vote majority vote, far less a sixty-vote, filibuster-proof majority.

The UK fixed health care annual budget is an effective, if harsh, mechanism to limit health care costs and maintain a stranglehold on health care inflation. Since the National Health Service is "free for all, from cradle to grave," funded through general taxation, and without stated limits on care, it is widely popular with the public. Only 11 percent of the British public have private health insurance, and this does not provide emergency services or provide the choice of an NHS general practitioner. The waiting lists in the United Kingdom are facts of life, and with the exception of the occasional high-publicity cases, they are tacitly accepted by the British public.

Such tacit acceptance would never fly in the United States: A single-payer, single-provider system in the United States, the VA medical system, was recently roundly criticized for lack of performance. It made national headlines when three hundred thousand US veterans were placed on waiting lists of three months, and a number died while awaiting care. This created a national outcry in the United States. In Britain, this is public policy. Why the stark contrast? The United States is a much larger and more diverse market, with much greater expectations than Britain. Waiting more than two weeks for a nonemergency elective surgery would not be acceptable in the United States; in Britain, this not only tolerated but expected.

The last ten years has seen a reining in of health care costs in the United States. This is primarily due to the 2008 recession when millions of Americans lost their health insurance.

Those who retained their insurance were in no mood to pay deductibles or out-of-pocket expenses.

Increasingly in the United States, physicians are electing to leave fee-for-service private practice and become salaried employees of the expanding hospital systems. A recent study by the AMA showed the proportion of physicians in private practice decreased by 10 percent per year over the last five years to a record low of 30 percent remaining in private practice in 2015. It is very unlikely that some form of the US fee-for-service model will ever be completely replaced since this would remove any and all motivation for the physician to be more productive or to work harder or longer. To remove all incentive from a reimbursement model in any profession, physician or not, shifts us to an NHS model without incentives, with all that that incurs.

Currently, the most sustainable systems in the new health care environment of the future are the Kaiser Permanentes, the major university systems, the Mayo Clinics and Cleveland Clinic systems and the community not-for-profit hospitals. These models represent the majority of health care delivery systems in the United States. In theory, employed physicians shift away from pure fee-for-service models, the much-vaunted source of health care inflation. On the flip side, the American public is in no mood to wait for months for an elective procedure, which in turn requires physicians to be proactive, aggressive, and hardworking in order to satisfy a consumer need.

In the United Kingdom, the single-payer, single-provider system, with a fixed budget, results in a low-cost, low-inflation system with limited procedures and fewer patient interactions, compared to a mostly consumer-driven, free-market system such as in the United States. A fixed-budget, controlled-cost, low-intervention system inevitably has lesser outcomes compared to a more liquid free-market system: higher mortality rates from cancer due to lack of screening; higher rates of death from myocardial infarction ("heart attack") due to lower cardiac intervention rates; higher hospital mortality due to limited funding and limited quality assurance programs. This is not a criticism. It is a financial and biological inevitability. Where these conflicting demands reach equilibrium depends on how society and the free market decides what it is willing to pay for and what limits it is prepared to accept.

In 2016, of the original twenty-three state co-operatives set up under the Affordable Care Act, sixteen have been closed by state insurance regulators, after clocking up an estimated $1.7 billion dollars in losses. Each of the remaining seven co-ops are operating in deficit, and have proposed staggering premium rate increases to remain afloat. It is ironic to look back six years at the inception of the Act, when the American public was reassured that each of these twenty-three plans had been carefully hand-picked for their "high probability of financial viability" and these plans were "plans for people, not for profit". Certainly they excelled in the latter goal of achieving "non-profit" status, and in fact amassed astronomical losses. But for the estimated 800,000 Americans left adrift without health insurance when their co-op closed its doors, the "plans for people" seems misplaced.

In the private health care insurance sector, the recent merger and acquisition frenzy will lead to three or four major private insurers dominating the health care insurance industry. These last men standing will also face strict government requirements under the ACA: guaranteed issue, no lifetime minimum, limited copays, limited insurance ratings, and a blizzard of legislative and administrative requirements.

In a very similar scenario to the housing market implosion, with its government interference, mandatory loan requirements, and vulnerability to political whim, these few men standing are now equally vulnerable to the same government attention. The government required mortgage lenders and banks to provide loans for affordable housing to those who could ill, or never, afford the loan payments, leading to the implosion of the housing sector. This, in turn, led to a credit crisis, the bankruptcy of Lehman Brothers, and government bailouts of AIG, GM, GMAC, and Chrysler. As impossible as a government bailout of the health care sector may seem, few, if any, predicted the identical catastrophe of 2008 prior to it happening.

A near-identical scenario played out in Britain prior to World War I and World War II. A diverse, pluralistic health care insurance sector imploded into government-run medicine after a global military, political, and financial upheaval. In the United States, the costs of the 2008 financial crisis dwarf the costs of the Vietnam War, Afghanistan, and Iraq wars combined. The aftermath may have the same political, economic, and social sequel, and the consequences will inevitably be the same: A single payer US national health service, with all of its second rate outcomes.

About the Author

DAVID N. ARMSTRONG, MD, A TRIPLE-BOARDED SURGEON, has operated for more than thirty years in Britain's National Health Service and in the US health-care system. He has worked in the Royal Infirmaries of Manchester and Edinburgh in the United Kingdom and Yale University and the Mayo Clinic in the United States.

Dr. Armstrong has had a front seat to the demise of the health service in Britain, and sees a similar fate for health care in the US.

In addition to a full time surgical practice, Dr. Armstrong has extensive scientific publications researching complex surgical conditions and is the pioneer of a number of innovative surgical devices and medications that are now used around the world.

His other contributions to the advancement of the study of medicine include creating the first colorectal fellowship program in the Southeast United States, in Atlanta GA. The program continues to provide training for the best and brightest doctors in America.

Dr. Armstrong is also a Fellow of the Royal College of Surgeons of Edinburgh, the American College of Surgeons and the American Society of Colorectal Surgeons. Dr. Armstrong lives and practices in Atlanta GA.

Printed in the United States
By Bookmasters